S0-AKH-402

GREATEST RECIPES

GREATEST RECIPES

a legendary combination
and great formula for

creative cooking

Colophon

www.rebo-publishers.com – info@rebo-publishers.com

Proofreading: Jarmila Peskova Skranakova, Joshua Joseph

Layout and cover design: Minkowski, bureau voor visuele communicatie, Enkhuizen, The Netherlands

ISBN 90 366 1568 2

contents

STARTERS

for **12** pizzas

Preparation

Dissolve the fresh yeast in water, add the flour, water, and oil then knead with the dough hook of an electric mixer for 5 minutes, or until smooth and elastic. Wash and chop the parsley and sorrel. Peel and chop the garlic. Knead the sorrel, parsley, and garlic into the dough. Cover and leave to rise in a warm place.

Divide into 12 balls, flatten them, and roll out thinly on a floured board.

Wash carrots, peel them, and cut into ¼-inch pieces. Heat the oil and sauté the carrots until half-cooked, about 5 minutes. Season with a pinch of salt. Wash the tomatoes, remove the cores, and cut into ½-inch thick slices. Wash the zucchini, trim the ends, and cut into ¼-inch thick slices. Drain and shred the mozzarella.

Cover 4 pizzas with zucchini, 4 with carrots, and 4 with tomatoes. Sprinkle all of them with the mozzarella, salt, and pepper and place on a greased cookie sheet. Bake in the oven. See below for baking times and temperatures.

Drizzle with oil and sprinkle with basil when cooked.

Serve hot.

Ingredients

For the yeast dough

4 tsp fresh yeast, 2–3 tbsp warm water

2⅓ cups whole-wheat flour

1 cup warm water, 1 tbsp corn oil

½ tsp salt, 1 bunch parsley

1 bunch sorrel, 2 cloves garlic

For the topping

6 carrots, 1 tbsp corn oil

3 cups small, firm tomatoes

6 small zucchinis, 11 oz mozzarella

salt, pepper, 4 tbsp corn oil

1 tbsp fresh chopped basil

Mini Pizzas

Oven

Conventional oven: 375–400 °F (preheated)

Fan-assisted oven: 350–375 °F (preheated)

Gas oven: Mark 3 (preheated)

Baking time: 25–30 minutes

Serves **4**

Preparation

Preheat oven to 400 °F. Cut off the mushroom stalks and chop finely along with two mushroom caps. Fry this mixture together with the scallions in the butter until soft. Take the pan off the heat and add tomato and breadcrumbs, and season according to taste with salt and pepper. Add half the grated cheese and mix well to complete the stuffing.

Brush the inside of the mushroom caps with pesto and carefully fill each cap with the stuffing. Place the caps on a waxed baking sheet and scatter the remaining grated cheese on top. Bake the caps just before serving for about 10 minutes in the oven (or until they are sufficiently hot and firm). Serve on small plates, with small forks.

For pesto: put the basil, garlic, pistachio nuts and Parmesan cheese in the food processor and mix until the mixture is finely chopped. Add the oil until the pesto acquires the desired thickness. Season with salt and pepper.

You can prepare the stuffed mushroom caps 8 hours in advance, and then bake them in the oven just before serving.

Mushroom Caps with Pesto Stuffing

Ingredients

14 mushrooms of similar size

4 scallions, finely chopped

1 tbsp unsalted butter

8 sun-dried tomatoes in oil, drained and finely chopped

1 tbsp dry breadcrumbs, salt and pepper

3 tbsp Parmesan cheese (grated)

4 tbsp pesto (ready-made or home-made; see right)

Ingredients for pesto

4–5 oz fresh basil leaves

2 garlic cloves, peeled

2 oz pistachio nuts, roasted

1 ¼ cups Parmesan cheese

⅔ cup olive oil

salt and pepper

Serves **8**

Preparation

Preheat oven to 350 °F. Grease eight large (volume 10 fl oz) muffin forms with some canola oil.

Heat the oil in a frying pan and fry the mushrooms, scallions and garlic for about 3 minutes over high heat. Allow the mixture to cool somewhat.

Put the mushroom mixture in a bowl, add cheddar cheese, ricotta cheese, eggs and nutmeg and season with salt and pepper.

Cut the slices of ham into small strips and add to the mushroom mixture.

Place the slices of filo pastry on top of one another, and cut them in half lengthwise. Cut each piece further into 4 pieces of equal size. Brush the four pieces of pastry with some canola oil and lay them in a muffin form; repeat for the other forms.

Spoon the stuffing into the forms with the pastry.

Bake the tarts for 20 to 25 minutes in the oven until golden- brown. Allow to cool for a few minutes; remove from the forms. Serve the tarts with crispy green salad.

Tarts with Ham and Mushrooms

Ingredients

1 tbsp canola oil, 1 tbsp olive oil

4 oz mushrooms, sliced

6 scallions, finely chopped

1 garlic clove, crushed

2 oz cheddar, grated

7 oz ricotta cheese, 2 eggs

¼ tsp nutmeg, black pepper

6 slices (4 oz) of ham, 4 sheets of filo pastry

12 pieces

Preparation

Mix the flour and the baking powder and sift into a bowl. Add grated cheese, eggs, salt, paprika powder, and sour cream. Beat all the ingredients with a hand-mixer equipped with a dough hook into a smooth mixture.

Transfer the dough to 12 greased muffin cups and place on a rack in the oven. See below for the baking time and temperatures.

Leave the muffins to cool in the pan for 10 minutes after baking. Then remove them and leave to cool on a rack.

Cheese **Muffins**

Ingredients

2 cups all-purpose flour

3 level tsp baking powder

2 cups grated sharp yellow cheese (Monterey Jack or Cheddar)

4 medium eggs

salt, sweet paprika powder

¾ cup sour cream

Oven

Conventional oven: around 350 °F (preheated)

Fan-assisted oven: around 325 °F (preheated)

Gas oven: Mark 3 (preheated)

Baking time: around 25 minutes

starters

Preparation

Scrape the asparagus stems to remove tough parts, trim, and wash. Bind them into 4 bundles with kitchen twine and place them in salted boiling water. Add the butter and sugar, bringing the asparagus to boil and cook for 15–20 minutes. Strain the asparagus, remove the kitchen twine, and arrange them on a buttered flameproof dish.

Dip the beefsteak tomatoes briefly in boiling water (don't let them cook), allow them to cool, slice in half, skin, core, scoop out the seeds, then cut the flesh into cubes. Peel and mince the shallots.

Melt the butter and fry the chopped shallots, add the cubed tomatoes and basil, and continue frying for 5 minutes. Season the mixture with pepper and spread over the asparagus.

Crumble the cheese finely with a fork, blend with the fresh cream, spread this mixture over the tomatoes and broil under a pre-heated broiler for about 5 minutes.

Ingredients

5 lbs large blanched asparagus

8 cups boiling salted water

1 tbsp butter, pinch of sugar

4 large beefsteak tomatoes

4 shallots, 4 tbsp butter

3 tbsp finely chopped basil leaves

6 oz blue cheese

2 ½ tbsp crème fraîche

white pepper

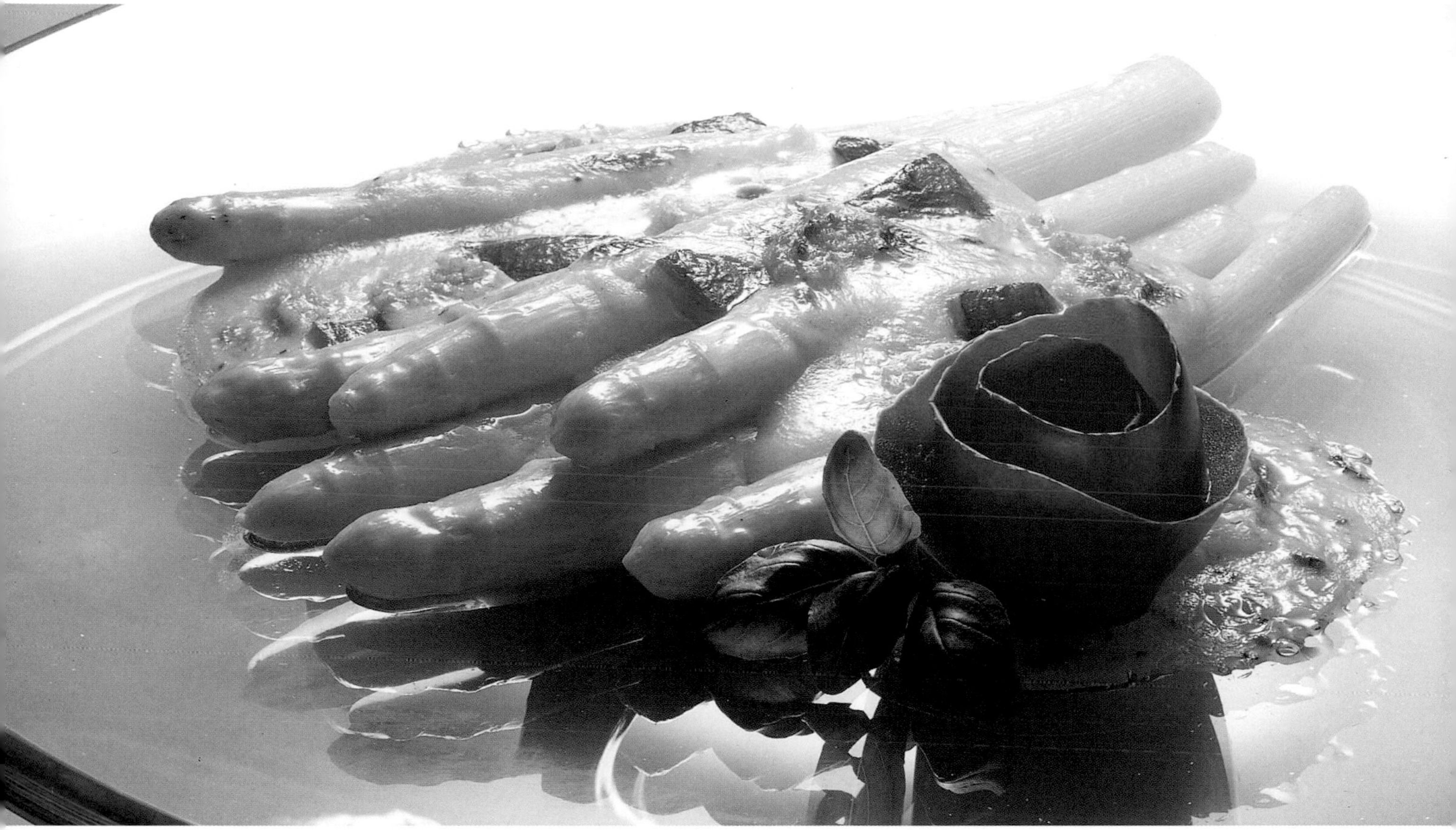

Asparagus au Gratin

starters

Tip

Serve with new potatoes.

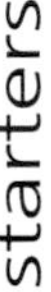

Serves **4**

Preparation

Preheat oven to 425 °F. Cut 4 circles 5 inches in diameter from the puff pastry. Make a ½-inch edge on the circles using a sharp knife. Place the pastry circles on a baking sheet.

Heat the oil in a large frying pan and fry the onion for about 10 minutes until soft. Add the chili pepper and fry for another minute. Season the onion mixture with salt and pepper.

Brush the pastry circles entirely with the pesto, except for the edges. Spoon the onion stuffing onto the pesto layer and scatter the pine nuts evenly over the circles.

Bake the tarts for 12 to 15 minutes until they have risen and are golden brown.

Red Onion **and Chili Pepper Tarts**

Ingredients

13 oz rolled -out puff pastry

1 tbsp olive oil

7 oz red onions, halved and chopped lengthwise

1 small red chili pepper, without seeds, chopped thinly

2 tbsp red pesto

1 tbsp pine nuts

salt and black pepper

starters

12 tomatoes

Preparation

Wash the tomatoes, pat dry, cut off the top and scoop out the pulp. Sprinkle the insides with salt and pepper.

Remove the mozzarella from its bag, reserving the liquid. Cut it into pieces and mix with the basil.

Mix the mozzarella liquid with olive oil and vinegar. Season with salt and pepper.

Pour this over the cheese mixture, leave it to soak in for a few minutes. Use the mixture to stuff the tomatoes. Garnish with basil leaves.

Serve with pita or ciabatta.

Italian Stuffed **Tomatoes**

Ingredients

12 cherry tomatoes, salt

freshly ground pepper

For the filling

3 packages mozzarella (4 oz each)

5 tbsp chopped fresh basil

5 tbsp mozzarella liquid

8 tbsp olive oil, 6 tbsp balsamic vinegar

salt, freshly ground white pepper

basil leaves

Tip

Add a peeled, crushed garlic clove to the marinade.

Serves **4**

Preparation

Preheat the oven to 350 °F.

Make triangles of the chicken wings and place them in a large roasting pan.

Mix the remaining ingredients, apart from the sesame seeds, in a bowl and pour over the chicken.

Roast the chicken wings for 25 to 30 minutes until brown and done. Rotate a few times during roasting. Take the chicken wings out of the oven and place them on a plate. Sprinkle with sesame seeds and serve immediately.

Chicken Wings with Fresh Ginger

Ingredients

2 ¼ lbs chicken wings

2 cloves garlic, crushed

½ tsp soy sauce, 2 tbsp oil, 2 tbsp sugar

4 tbsp fresh ginger, grated

3 tbsp sherry

2 tbsp roasted sesame seeds

Serves **4–6**

Preparation

Break off the hard base of the asparagus.

Cook the asparagus for 4 minutes in boiling water until they become tender but still crisp.

Rinse with cold water and pat dry with paper towels.

Pour the lemon juice in a bowl for the dressing.

Add the oil slowly and allow the mixture to thicken while stirring.

Season the dressing with salt and pepper.

Pour the dressing over the asparagus and serve with Pecorino shavings and the pieces of pancetta.

Ingredients

1 lb 2 oz fresh asparagus

juice of 1 lemon

⅜ cup olive oil, extra virgin

Pecorino cheese shavings

8 thin slices of pancetta, in pieces

freshly ground pepper

sea salt

Asparagus with Pecorino and Pancetta

Serves **4–6**

Preparation

Preheat oven to 400 °F. Slice all potatoes in half and mix them with the oil in a bowl. Season with salt and pepper and place them with the sliced end facing down on a greased baking sheet. Bake for about 20 minutes until they are soft. Leave potatoes to cool.

Mix, in the meantime, the finely cut salmon, sour cream, onions, horseradish and chives in a small bowl and add salt and pepper. Create a small hollow in the potato halves and slice the top of the round ends so that they can stand upright. Stuff the potatoes with a teaspoon of the salmon stuffing and place them on a serving dish.

Garnish each potato with a small square of salmon, some salmon caviar and finely chopped chives.

Place them in the fridge to chill for about 2 hours before serving.

New Potatoes with Smoked Salmon

Ingredients

24 new potatoes, 1 tbsp olive oil, salt and pepper

5 oz smoked salmon, finely cut

3 tbsp sour cream

2 tbsp Bermuda onions, finely chopped

1 tsp white horseradish

a small bag fresh chives, finely chopped

2 oz thinly sliced smoked salmon (in 24 small squares)

capers, salmon caviar, and extra sprigs of chive for garnishing

Serves **4**

Preparation

Put the mustard in a bowl, add vinegar, sugar, salt, pepper and herbs. Mix well. Add olive oil while stirring.

Cover the bowl and set aside the vinaigrette until needed.

Steam the asparagus for 5 to 10 minutes until just tender, but ensure that they are still crisp.

Place the asparagus on a plate and sprinkle them with the vinaigrette. Serve hot or cold.

Asparagus with Vinaigrette

Ingredients

1 tbsp Dijon mustard

4 tbsp red wine vinegar

½ tsp sugar, ¼ tsp salt

¼ tsp freshly ground black pepper

fresh parsley, finely chopped

fresh chives, finely chopped

⅜ cup olive oil, 1 bundle of asparagus

starters

Serves **6**

Preparation

Chill the melons for a few hours, cut them in half, remove the seeds, and cut each half into 6 slices.

Place a slice of ham on each slice of melon and sprinkle with freshly ground black pepper.

Ingredients

2 ripe honeydew or crenshaw melons

12 thin slices Parma ham

freshly ground black pepper

Melon with Parma Ham

Tip

Serve melon and parma ham as an appetizer or light evening meal.

Serves **6**

Preparation

Brush a sheet of waxed baking paper with oil and sprinkle with salt and pepper.

Place four slices of beef, approximately 2 inches from one another, on the baking paper. Place on top of this another sheet of oiled baking paper and beat until the beef has doubled in size. Put the meat in the fridge until ready for use.

Place some arugula in the middle of a plate and arrange the slices of beef around it. Sprinkle with balsamic vinegar, olive oil, Pecorino and pepper.

Beef Carpaccio

Ingredients

1 tbsp oil

1 lb beef fillet in slices ¼ inch thick

4 oz arugula, washed

1 ½ tbsp balsamic vinegar

¼ cup olive oil, extra virgin

Pecorino shavings

salt and freshly ground black pepper

starters

Preparation

Rinse the eggplants, cut it into 1-inch slices, and dice. Soak in salted water for 10 minutes and pat dry. Wash, dry, and mince the parsley.

Heat the oil in a skillet and sauté the eggplants until golden brown, turning occasionally. Add the sieved tomatoes.

Peel and chop the garlic and add to the mixture. Season with salt, pepper, and oregano. Bring the mixture briefly to a boil, then remove from the heat and cool to room temperature. Sprinkle with the parsley before serving.

Ingredients

3 large eggplants

vegetable oil

½ cup sieved, canned tomatoes

2 cloves garlic

freshly ground pepper

½ tsp dried oregano

½ bunch flat-leaf parsley

salt

Marinated **Eggplants**

Serves **4**

Preparation

Slice the top and bottom off 1 of the oranges, then cut away the peel and core, following the curve of the fruit. Cut between the membranes to release the segments, then chop roughly. Squeeze the juice of the other orange into a bowl, add the chopped orange, tomatoes, garlic, vinegar and 3 tablespoons of the oil, then season.

Heat a ridged cast-iron grill pan or heavy-based frying pan. Brush both sides of each fennel slice with half the remaining oil. Cook for 2–3 minutes on each side until tender and charred. Transfer to serving plates and keep warm.

Brush the scallops with the remaining oil and cook for 1 minute, then turn and cook for 30 seconds or until cooked through. Top the fennel with 1 tablespoon of crème fraîche, 3 scallops and the salsa.

Serve with the rocket leaves (or watercress).

Griddled Scallops with Orange Salsa

Ingredients

2 small oranges
4 sun-dried tomatoes in oil, drained and chopped
1 clove garlic, crushed
1 tbsp balsamic vinegar
4 tbsp extra virgin olive oil
salt and black pepper
1 large head fennel, cut lengthways into 8 slices
12 fresh prepared scallops
4 tbsp crème fraîche
rocket leaves (or watercress) to serve

Serves **4–6**

Preparation

Scrub the mussels well and remove beard. Dispose of any open or damaged mussels. Put the mussels in a large pan with the wine and garlic. Place a lid on the pan and cook for 3 minutes over high heat until they open. Shake the pan regularly. Throw the still closed mussels away.

Remove the upper shell of each mussel.

Mix all the ingredients for the garlic butter in a bowl. Place the mixture in the shells and broil until the mussels start to sizzle.

Serve with freshly baked baguette.

Mussel Escargot

Ingredients

2 ¼ lbs mussels

⅝ cup dry white wine

2 cloves garlic, crushed

For the garlic butter

1 lb 2 oz soft butter

2 cloves garlic, chopped

1 tbsp fresh parsley, chopped

⅛ cup cognac, salt and pepper

Serves **6**

Preparation

Sprinkle the oysters with lime juice and top with smoked salmon.

Put a dollop of the sour cream onto each oyster.

Garnish with chives and red caviar.

Serve on a bed of ice.

Ingredients

3 dozen natural oysters in shells

juice of ½ lime or lemon

6 slices smoked salmon (cut into fine strips)

1 cup sour cream

2 tbsp fresh chives chopped for garnish

red caviar for garnish

crushed ice for serving

Oysters **Greta Garbo**

Serves **2**

Preparation

Thaw the scallops. Make sure to cut jumbo scallops in half.

Rinse and pat dry with paper towels.

Heat butter or margarine in a skillet over medium-high heat.

Add the green onion and cook and stir for 1 minute. Then move the onion to one side.

Add scallops and tarragon. Cook onion and scallops for 5 to 6 minutes or until scallops are opaque and most of the liquid has evaporated, stirring frequently.

Stir in dry white wine.

Scallops Tarragon

Ingredients

1 lb mixed or jumbo scallops

2 tbsp butter or margarine

¼ cup sliced green onion

¼ tsp dried tarragon, crushed

1 tbsp dry white wine

12 pieces

Preparation

Combine soy sauce, Worcestershire sauce, and honey in a small bowl and set aside.

Wrap a bacon strip around each oyster, then thread 2 wrapped oysters onto each skewer. Place skewers in a foil-lined grill pan. Pour marinade over oysters, cover and leave for 30 minutes.

Cook oysters under a preheated grill until bacon is golden.

Serve immediately.

Ingredients

2 tbsp soy sauce

½ tsp Worcestershire sauce

1 tbsp honey

4 strips rindless back bacon, cut into three 1 ¼ in strips

2 dozen oysters, shells discarded

12 small wooden skewers

Oysters **Marinated with Bacon**

starters

Serves **4**

Preparation

Remove the oysters from their shells and place in the fridge. Wash the shells and arrange them on four oven-proof plates over a layer of sea salt. Heat the butter in a pan and fry the leek while stirring. Season with salt, pepper and sugar. Cover the pan well and leave to simmer. Sprinkle with lemon juice.

Bring the wine with the saffron and curry powder to a boil and boil until reduced to half. Mix the cream with the egg yolk in a bowl and add this to the wine mixture. Stir continuously until the sauce thickens somewhat (it must not boil). Add salt and pepper and take the pan from the heat.

Spoon some finely chopped leek into each shell and place the oysters on top. Pour the sauce over the oysters and place them under a preheated broiler for several minutes until they are sautéed. Serve immediately.

Spicy Oysters with Leek

Ingredients

20–24 large oysters in the shell

granulated sea salt

1 tbsp butter

1 thin leek, finely chopped

salt

freshly ground pepper and some sugar

freshly-squeezed lemon juice

⅓ cup dry white wine

a few saffron threads or a pinch of curry powder

⅔ cup cream

1 egg yolk

SOUPS

Serves **4**

Preparation

Place cucumber, pineapple, mango, red pepper, tomatoes, green onion, mint, coriander, tomato and pineapple juices, Worcestershire sauce and tabasco sauce to taste in a glass bowl. Mix to combine. Cover. Refrigerate overnight or until cold.

For salsa: place avocado, coriander and lime juice in a bowl. Mix to combine. Cover. Refrigerate until ready to use. Best used within a few days of making.

Ladle soup into chilled bowls, to serve. Top with a spoonful of salsa.

Ingredients

½ cup finely diced cucumber
½ cup finely diced pineapple
½ cup finely diced mango
¼ red pepper, finely diced
2 plum tomatoes, finely diced
1 green onion, chopped
2 tbsp chopped fresh mint
2 tbsp chopped fresh coriander
1 cup tomato or vegetable juice
1 cup pineapple juice
1 tsp no-added-salt Worcestershire sauce
tabasco sauce, to taste

Caribbean Gazpacho
with Avocado Salsa

For the Avocado Salsa

1 avocado, diced

1 tbsp chopped fresh coriander

1 tsp lime juice

Preparation

Simmer the ham hock, 12 cups water, lentils, ginger and garlic in a large pan for an hour. Stir in the carrot, onion, turmeric and chili and simmer for 30 minutes.

Transfer the ham to a cutting board, remove meat from bones and chop. Add the meat to the pan with the vinegar, salt and pepper to taste then simmer, uncovered, for 30 minutes. Stir in the chopped coriander and season with salt and pepper.

Ladle soup into bowls, discarding the ginger, and garnish with coriander leaves.

Lentil Soup with Coriander

Ingredients

1 lb 2 oz ham hock

2 cups lentils

3 slices ginger

1 clove garlic, crushed

2 carrots, grated

1 onion, chopped

2 tsp turmeric

½ tsp chili powder

2 tbsp white vinegar

2 tbsp chopped coriander

whole coriander leaves to garnish

Serves **6**

Preparation

Mix the white beans, kidney beans and chickpeas together and soak in cold water overnight (if you don't have time to soak the beans overnight, cover them with hot water for two hours then drain and proceed with the recipe).

Sauté the onions and garlic in the olive oil for 5 minutes or until soft. Add the cabbage, celery and carrots and sauté for a further 5 minutes or until the vegetables have softened.

Add the beef stock, tomato paste, soaked bean mixture, basil, parsley, bay leaves plus salt and pepper to taste. Simmer for 2 hours or until thick and fragrant. Add the Parmesan cheese rind, sliced zucchini, red wine and a little extra water if necessary to thin the soup. Cook for a further 30 minutes, remove bay leaves and serve.

Ingredients

½ cup small white beans
½ cup kidney beans
½ cup chickpeas
4 white onions, chopped
2 cloves garlic, minced
3 tbsp olive oil
½ small cabbage, sliced
2 ribs celery, sliced
2 medium carrots, sliced finely

6 cups good quality beef stock
2 tbsp tomato paste
12 basil leaves, chopped
6 sprigs parsley
3 bay leaves (fresh if possible)
⅔ cup piece Parmesan rind
4 zucchinis, sliced
1 cup good red wine
salt and pepper to taste

Minestrone Piemonte

Tip

A particularly nice touch is to finish each bowl with a spoonful of pesto. The heat of the soup warms the pesto and causes it to permeate the entire bowl of soup.

Serves **6**

Preparation

Peel and finely chop the shallots and onions. Peel the garlic cloves. Heat the olive oil and butter then, when foaming, add the shallots and onions and cook over a high heat until golden, about 5 minutes. Reduce the heat to low and add the garlic cloves, continuing to cook for 30 minutes until the onion/garlic mixture is deep golden; do not allow the garlic to burn.

Slice the baguette into 6 neat slices and set aside. Cut the remaining crust off the baguette and break the inner soft bread into little pieces (you should have about a half a cup). Tie the herbs together with cooking string then add the stock and herbs to the soup, along with salt and pepper to taste; bring to a boil. Add the bread pieces and simmer the soup for 20 minutes. Remove the herbs then add the milk and cream and gently purée the soup until smooth.

Brush the remaining baguette slices with a little olive oil and sprinkle with the paprika. Grill until golden on both sides. To serve, place one of the grilled bread slices in each bowl and ladle over the hot soup. Garnish with chopped chives.

New Orleans **Garlic Soup**

Ingredients

6 shallots
2 brown onions
2 large heads garlic
1 tbsp olive oil
1 tbsp butter
1 baguette (French bread)
6 sprigs parsley
5 sprigs thyme
4 sprigs oregano
2 fresh bay leaves
4 cups vegetable stock
¾ cup milk
⅔ cup pure cream
1 tbsp olive oil
2 tsp mild paprika
1 bunch chives, chopped
salt and lots of freshly ground pepper

Serves **6**

Preparation

Put the shiitake mushrooms in an ovenproof bowl, add 1 cup boiling water and allow to stand for 25 minutes or until the mushrooms are soft. Drain, then strain and reserve the liquid. Cut the mushrooms into thin slices.

Put the stock, mushroom liquid, ginger, garlic, star anise and soy sauce into a large pot and bring to a boil. Reduce the heat and simmer for 10 minutes. Remove the ginger, garlic and star anise and discard.

Add the oyster mushrooms, dried shiitake, Udon noodles and spring onions and simmer gently for 5 minutes.

Stir in the enoki and heat for 1 minute or until they soften. Serve hot.

Ingredients

8 dried shiitake mushrooms
4 cups reduced salt vegetable stock
1 in piece ginger, crushed
1 halved garlic clove
1 whole star anise
1 tbsp soy sauce
1 cup oyster mushrooms
14 oz fresh Udon noodles
3 spring onions, sliced
1 cup enoki mushrooms, gently separated

Mixed Mushroom **Noodle Soup**

Serves **6–8**

Preparation

Place mushrooms and onions in a large, heavy based saucepan. Add water, salt and lemon juice and bring slowly to a boil. Lower heat, cover and simmer gently for 1 ½ hours.

Strain liquid through a fine sieve and return to clean saucepan. Add Madeira or sherry and season to taste with black pepper. Heat through and serve with garnishes.

Ingredients

2 lb mushrooms, roughly chopped

2 lb onions, chopped

8 cups water

1 tbsp fresh lemon juice

5 tbsp Madeira or dry sherry

1 tsp salt

freshly ground black pepper

Mushroom & Onion **Consomme**

For garnish

thin julienne strips; spring onion

finely sliced button mushrooms;

finely sliced radish;

6–8 sprigs fresh watercress

Serves **6–8**

Preparation

Heat the olive oil and sauté the chopped shallots, Spanish onion, garlic and thyme until softened. Add the chopped tomatoes and tomato paste then sauté for a further 2 minutes.

Add the vegetable stock, sugar, salt and pepper to taste and bring to a boil. Simmer for 25 minutes then purée with a hand-held "wand" or in a food processor. The soup should be thick enough to support the garnish. If it seems a little thin, simmer for a further 10 minutes to reduce.

Prepare the garnish. Quarter all the tiny tomatoes (if using) and finely slice the basil leaves with a very sharp knife. In a separate bowl, crumble the feta cheese and set aside.

To serve the soup, divide into deep bowls then heavily garnish with a pile of chopped tomatoes, basil leaves and feta cheese.

Summer Garden Tomato Soup

Ingredients

1 tbsp olive oil

2 shallots

1 large Spanish onion, chopped

2 cloves garlic, minced

2 large sprigs thyme

3 lb 6 oz of summer tomatoes, either red or yellow, roughly chopped

2 tbsp tomato paste (omit if using yellow tomatoes)

2 cups vegetable stock

1 tbsp sugar

2 baskets assorted tiny tomatoes, chopped (optional)

⅔ cup feta cheese, finely crumbled

1 bunch basil

salt and pepper to taste

soups

Preparation

Trim and wash the cauliflower flowerets. Wash and chop the carrots. Shell and wash the beans. Wash the leeks and cut them into ½-inch pieces. Wash and chop the celery. Wash peas.

Melt the butter and sauté the vegetables. Add the broth and season with salt and pepper. Bring to a boil and simmer for 20 minutes.

Dip the tomatoes in boiling water (do not cook), then plunge into cold water. Remove the skins and core and chop them. Add them to the soup. Sprinkle the soup with the herbs before serving.

Serving suggestion: Farina dumplings

Country Vegetable Soup

Ingredients

1 cup cauliflower flowerets

2 medium carrots

½ cup fresh green beans

1 large stick celery

⅔ cup shelled garden peas

3 tbsp butter

1 leek

3 cups vegetable broth

2 medium tomatoes

2 tbsp freshly chopped herbs (such as parsley, chervil, and thyme)

freshly ground pepper

salt

Preparation

Wash the fresh spinach, and cook for a few minutes in a saucepan without added water until it wilts. Heat frozen spinach without thawing, stirring until it boils. Drain in sieve and leave to cool. Squeeze out excess water. Chop and heat again with 1 tablespoon butter and salt. Leave to cool. Stir in the eggs, 3 tablespoons Parmesan cheese and a pinch of grated nutmeg.

Heat the beef broth, add the spinach, cover, and remove from heat. Let stand for a few minutes, so the eggs can bind the soup.

Fry the bread in the remaining butter until golden brown. Pour the soup into warmed soup bowls and serve with remaining cheese.

Spinach Soup

Ingredients

6 cups chopped spinach leaves

or 2 cups frozen spinach

4 tbsp butter

2 medium eggs

salt, grated nutmeg

⅔ cup Parmesan cheese

4 cups beef broth

3 slices Italian-style bread

soups

Serves **4**

Preparation

Heat the oil in a big pot. Peel and chop the onions and sauté them in the oil. Wash the leek under cold running water and drain well. Cut the leek in slices and add these to the onions, sautéing them together for 5 minutes.

Rinse the rice in cold running water, drain well, then add to the vegetables. Add the vegetable broth, then the bay leaf and rosemary. Season well with salt, pepper, and grated nutmeg. Reduce the heat and simmer the soup on low heat for 20–25 minutes.

Mix the milk and flour, add to the soup, and cook for 5 minutes. Mix the egg yolk with yogurt. Remove the soup from the fire and thicken it with the yogurt mix. Once again season the rice soup. Before serving, mix in the rinsed and finely chopped mint.

Rice Soup with Mint

Ingredients

2 tbsp olive oil
1 onion
1 leek
⅔ cup rice
2 cups vegetable broth
1 bay leaf
1 sprig rosemary
grated nutmeg
⅔ cup milk
1 tbsp all-purpose flour
2–3 egg yolks
⅔ cup yogurt
1 bunch fresh mint
freshly ground pepper
salt

Preparation

Wash the chicken under running water. Clean the inside of the chicken and place it, with the heart and neck, in a deep pot of salted boiling water. As broth returns to a boil, skim the surface.

Chop the soup vegetables, and add them to the soup. Peel the onion and add it to the pot. Cover and simmer the chicken in the broth for about 90 minutes. Strain the soup and add salt to taste.

Remove the meat from the bones, discard the skin, and cut the meat into small pieces.

Add the asparagus pieces, rice, and chicken pieces to the broth. Reheat it, skimming the surface with absorbent paper towel to remove excess fat. Sprinkle with minced parsley before serving.

Ingredients

1 boiling chicken (around 2 ½ lb)

6 cups boiling salted water

1 bunch soup vegetables (carrot, turnip, rutabaga)

1 medium onion

2 cups cooked asparagus

½ cup cooked long-grain rice

2 tbsp minced parsley

salt

Chicken Soup with Rice

Serves **4**

Preparation

Sauté the onions and mushrooms over a high heat until the onions are golden and the mushrooms are brown. Add garlic and stir for a minute. Add fish stock, chopped tomatoes and the juice reserved from the can of tomatoes. Stir in the bay leaf, rosemary, oregano, and hot peppers. Bring to a boil, then reduce heat and simmer, partially covered, for 25 minutes.

Add the zucchini chunks, cover, and simmer another 10 minutes until the zucchini is almost tender. Then slip the oysters with their liquid into the soup and cook, uncovered, just until their edges begin to curl. They should be tender, not chewy.

Ladle immediately into bowls. Sprinkle with parsley and serve immediately. Fat, dense oyster biscuits are delicious in this soup.

Manhattan Oyster **Chowder**

Ingredients

2 tbsp olive oil

1 onion, chopped into bite-sized chunks

¼ pound dark-gilled mushrooms, quartered

2 cloves garlic, chopped

3 cups fish stock

14-oz can of tomatoes, seeded and chopped

1 zucchini, cut into eighths and cut into bite-sized chunks

¼ tsp rosemary, crushed to a powder

¼ tsp oregano, crushed to a powder

pinch hot pepper flakes

1 pint standard oysters

parsley

bay leaf

Serves **6**

Preparation

Heat the fish broth. Rinse the fish under cold, running water, pat dry, and cut into small chunks. Simmer in the broth for 3 minutes; remove from broth, and reserve. Wash the vegetables, cut green onions into rings, and slice the fennel and bell peppers into strips. Chop the fennel fronds and set aside for garnishing.

Melt the butter, sauté the vegetables, and dust with flour. Add white wine, vermouth and broth, then reduce. Cook for 10 minutes, season with salt, pepper, and lemon juice. Add the heavy cream and crème fraîche.

Heat the fish, mussels, and shrimp in the soup, sprinkle with fennel fronds and serve.

Fish Soup with Fennel

Ingredients

4 cups fish or vegetable broth

7 oz salmon fillet; 7 oz red snapper fillet

2 green onions (scallions); 2 fennel bulbs

2 red bell peppers

2 tbsp butter

2 tbsp all-purpose flour

1 scant cup dry white wine

1 scant cup dry white vermouth

salt, freshly ground pepper

lemon juice; 1 cup heavy cream

⅔ cup crème fraîche

2 cups canned, shelled mussels

1 cup cooked, shelled shrimp

Tip

Fish soup can be made with a variety of freshwater and saltwater lean fish. Recommended varieties include cod, scrod, porgy, catfish, red snapper, redfish, weakfish, sole, and sand dabs.

Serves **4**

Preparation

Melt the butter in a saucepan and sauté the chicory. Remove the mussels from their shells and set the flesh apart. Add bouillon, cream and basil and beat together until well-blended. Add salt and pepper to taste. Add the mussels and cook until they are warmed through. Serve the mussels in bowls.

Mussel Soup with Chicory and Basil

Ingredients

2 tbsp butter

2 bunches chicory (or endive), leaves separated

1 cup bouillon made from the liquid used to cook the mussels, strained

2 tbsp cream

15 basil leaves, chopped fine

2 lbs black mussels in their shells (cooked à la marinière)

salt and pepper, according to taste

Serves **6**

Preparation

Heat the oil in a wok. Add the onion, tom yum, Venus clams and mussels; bring to a boil and simmer with the lid on for 30 seconds.

Pour the bouillon over the seafood; add lemongrass, lime juice, cilantro and Thai fish sauce and stir thoroughly. Simmer until all the mussels open. Discard any mussels that fail to open.

Add the cilantro leaves and serve in a soup bowl.

Mussel and Venus Clam Bouillon

Ingredients

3 tbsp vegetable oil

1 onion, finely chopped

2 tbsp tom yum paste

2 oz ready to cook Venus clams in their shells

7 oz ready to cook black mussels in their shells

½ cup chicken stock

1 stalk lemongrass, finely chopped

1 tbsp cilantro leaves, finely chopped

1 tbsp cilantro stalks and root, finely chopped

1 tbsp Thai fish sauce

juice of 1 lime

soups

Serves **4**

Preparation

Rinse the mussels in plenty of cold water, then brush them thoroughly, remove the beards, and rinse until the water is completely clear. Discard any mussels that open during rinsing and brushing. Peel and chop the onions. Clean the carrots and turnips, rinse them, and slice thinly. Bring water and white wine to a boil; add the onion and vegetables, add pepper and salt to taste, and boil for around 3 minutes.

Add the mussels and bring to a boil again, cover with the lid, and leave to cook for 10 minutes, or until the shells open (discard any mussels that remain unopened).

Strain the mussel cooking liquid through a cheesecloth-lined sieve and transfer the liquid to a pan. Remove the flesh from the shells and reserve. Stir the rinsed and minced parsley and the heavy cream into the cooking liquid.

Cut the cheese into small cubes and add it to the soup together with the mussel flesh. Reheat the soup, but do not let it boil. Season to taste and serve immediately.

Dutch Mussel Soup

Ingredients

3 lb 5 oz mussels

2 medium onions

2 carrots

2 turnips

2 cups water

1 cup dry white wine

salt

white pepper

1 bunch parsley

½ cup heavy cream

1 cup mature cheddar or Jack cheese

Tip

Serve with French bread.

soups

Serves **6**

Preparation

Blend milk, cream, butter or margarine, salt, pepper and Worcestershire sauce in the top of a double boiler. Place top of double boiler over the bottom with boiling water and bring to a simmer, stirring frequently. Add scallops to the mixture and cook until tender, about 8 to 10 minutes. Pour hot soup into individual bowls.

Sprinkle each bowl with paprika and parsley.

Rich Scallop Soup

Ingredients

1 lb scallops, chopped into small pieces

2 cups milk

1 cup heavy cream

2 tbsp butter or margarine

1 tsp salt

¼ tsp white pepper

1 tsp Worcestershire sauce

3 tbsp fresh parsley, finely chopped

paprika

soups

Serves **6**

Preparation

Heat the oil in a large pot, add the onion and cook over medium heat for 3 minutes or until the onion is soft and golden. Add the spices and chili and cook until fragrant, about 2 minutes. Stir in the tomatoes, chickpeas and fish stock and bring to a boil. Reduce the heat and simmer uncovered for 15 minutes.

Add the fish and cook for 5 minutes or just until the flesh is tender. Remove the soup from the heat, then add the couscous and cover. Set aside for 10 minutes or until the couscous is soft.

Serve with a dollop of yogurt and sprinkle with parsley and mint. Accompany with wedges of pita bread.

Spiced Fish, Tomato and Chickpea Soup

Ingredients

1 tbsp olive oil
1 onion, chopped
1 tsp ground coriander
1 tsp ground cumin
1 tsp allspice
1 green chili, finely sliced
1 14-oz can chopped tomatoes
1 14-oz can chickpeas, rinsed and drained
4 cups reduced salt fish stock
1 lb firm white fish fillets (redfish, bream, sea perch), cut into large pieces
thick, reduced fat natural yogurt, to serve
1 tbsp chopped fresh parsley
1 tbsp chopped fresh mint
pita bread, to serve
⅓ cup couscous

SALADS

Serves **4**

Preparation

Cook oysters in their own juice until the edges curl up. Drain and chill.

Place a lettuce leaf on 4 salad plates. Shred rest of lettuce and place on lettuce leaves.

Lay 6 oysters on each lettuce leaf and sprinkle with lemon juice.

Place tomato and celery on top. Dab oysters with mayonnaise; sprinkle with paprika, and chill for 1 hour before serving.

Ingredients

24 oysters, on the half shell or meat only

2 tomatoes, sliced thinly

6 tsp lemon juice

1 cup celery, diced

mayonnaise

paprika

lettuce

Oyster Salad

Serves **4**

Preparation

To make dressing: place mayonnaise, olive oil, vinegar and mustard in a bowl; mix to combine and set aside.

Heat sesame oil in a frying pan over high heat, add garlic and scallops and cook, stirring for 1 minute or until scallops turn just opaque. Remove scallop mixture from pan and set aside. Add bacon to pan and cook, stirring for 4 minutes or until crisp. Remove bacon from pan and drain on absorbent paper towel.

Place lettuce leaves in a large salad bowl, add dressing and toss to coat. Add bacon, croutons and shavings of Parmesan cheese; toss. Spoon scallop mixture over salad and serve.

Seared Scallop Salad

Ingredients

2 tsp sesame oil

2 cloves garlic, crushed

12 oz scallops, cleaned

4 slices bacon, chopped

1 head romaine lettuce, leaves separated

fresh Parmesan cheese

2 oz croutons

Mustard dressing

3 tbsp mayonnaise

1 tbsp olive oil

1 tbsp vinegar

2 tsp Dijon mustard

Serves **4–6**

Preparation

Place water, carrot, cauliflower, bell pepper, onion, saffron and cilantro seeds in a large saucepan. Bring the water to a boil and add the vinegar. Remove the saucepan from the heat immediately and let the marinade cool down. Remove the vegetables with a slotted spoon, keep apart and throw the cooking water away. **Mix** the mesclun salad, tomato, olive oil, vegetables and mussels together and add salt and pepper to taste.

Mussel Salad

Ingredients

Marinade:

1 ¼ cup water

1 small carrot, cubed

2 oz cauliflower, in florets

½ red bell pepper, minced

½ onion, minced

pinch saffron

10 cilantro seeds, crushed

3 tbsp sherry vinegar

10 oz cooked mussels

(approx. 2 lbs mussels in their shells)

Ingredients for the salad:

handful mesclun salad

a few cherry tomatoes halved

3 tbsp extra virgin olive oil

salt and pepper

Serves **4**

Preparation

To make dressing: place ginger, rosemary, garlic, oil, lime juice and vinegar in a screwtop jar and shake well to combine. Set aside.

Preheat barbecue to high heat. Place red and yellow or green pepper halves, skin side down on lightly oiled barbecue grill and cook for 5–10 minutes or until skins are blistered and charred. Place peppers in a plastic food bag or paper bag and set aside until cool enough to handle. Remove skins from peppers and cut flesh into thin strips.

Cut squid (calamari) tubes lengthwise and open out flat. Using a sharp knife cut parallel lines down the length of the squid (calamari), taking care not to cut through the flesh. Make more cuts in the opposite direction to form a diamond pattern. Cut into 2 in squares.

Place squid (calamari) and scallops on lightly oiled barbecue plate (griddle) and cook, turning several times, for 3 minutes or until tender. Set aside to cool slightly.

Combine red and yellow or green peppers, asparagus, onion and coriander. Line a large serving platter with rocket (or watercress) – top with vegetables, squid (calamari) and scallops. Drizzle with dressing and serve immediately.

Squid and Scallop Salad

Ingredients

1 red pepper, seeded and halved

1 yellow or green pepper, seeded

2 squid (calamari) tubes

8 oz scallops, roe (coral) removed

8 oz asparagus, cut into 2-in pieces, blanched

1 red onion, sliced

3 tbsp fresh coriander leaves

1 bunch rocket (or watercress)

Herb and balsamic dressing

1 tbsp finely grated fresh ginger

1 tbsp chopped fresh rosemary

1 clove garlic, crushed

¼ cup olive oil

2 tbsp lime juice

1 tbsp balsamic or red wine vinegar

Serves **6**

Preparation

Place scallops in a bowl with the oil and marinade 1 hour.

Divide greens amongst the plates—set fruit aside.

Shake vinaigrette ingredients together in a jar.

Add olive oil to a heavy based wok or frying pan and quickly toss-fry scallops on medium to high heat until seared very light brown, about 30 seconds (but don't crowd them or they will stew).

Spoon scallops over salad greens, scatter strawberries and apple cubes throughout, shake vinaigrette and drizzle.

Sprinkle with chives and serve immediately.

Note: Other berries (such as raspberries) can be used when in season.

Salad of Scallops on Bitter Greens with Strawberries

Ingredients

1 lb 2 oz scallops

3 tbsp of liver oil

Salad greens—enough watercress, iceberg, rocket, mizuna, chicory or yellow section of endive to cover the base of 6 entree plates

1 granny smith apple, unpeeled, in very small cubes or slices (squeeze a lemon over to prevent browning)

About 20 smallish strawberries, washed and halved

2 tbsp chopped chives (finely cut)

Vinaigrette

12 tbsp olive oil

3 tbsp raspberry vinegar

salt and pepper

salads

Serves **4**

Preparation

Place the squid rings on paper towel and dry.

Heat the oil in a skillet, add the shrimp and garlic and stir-fry 2 minutes over medium heat. Add the squid and stir-fry another 2 minutes. Set aside and cool.

Place the spinach, onion, pepper, peas, mint and nuts in a bowl or on a plate. Distribute the seafood on top.

Prepare the dressing, mixing chili sauce, soy sauce, lime juice and oil in a bowl.

Pour the dressing over the salad and cool.

Ingredients

¾ lb squid rings

1 tbsp olive oil

¾ lb medium-sized raw shrimp, peeled and deveined

1 clove garlic, pressed, 1 lb spinach

1 red onion, cut in rings

1 red pepper, cut in strips

9 oz (snow) peas, cleaned

2 tbsp fresh mint leaves

1 oz nuts, finely chopped

Chili dressing:

2 tbsp sweet chili sauce

1 tbsp soy sauce

1 tbsp lime juice

1 tbsp vegetable oil

Seafood Salad

Serves **2**

Preparation

Mix the salad of endive, cucumber, and tomatoes in a large bowl, and dress with a little oil, fruit juice and vinegar; season.

Fry the bacon in a little olive oil on low heat until crispy. Remove and set aside on some paper towel.

Fry the scallops in the bacon fat for only a few minutes on each side, they should adopt a lovely golden color; season them lightly, and squeeze in the remaining fruit juice. Turn off the heat.

Put some salad on a plate, and place a few scallops on top. Break up the bacon and scatter the pieces over. Pour over some of the juices from the pan and serve. For a bit of a twist you could serve small portions of this in the scallop shells.

Scallop and Bacon Salad

Ingredients

8 scallops, shells removed

3 slices bacon

olive oil

juice of 1 lemon/lime

salt and pepper

vinegar

a few good handfuls endive

cucumber, diced

cherry tomatoes, quartered

salads

Preparation

Wash the lettuce and arrange it on a plate. Drain the tuna, break into chunks with a fork, and arrange on the lettuce.

Peel the onion and slice it into rings. Toss it on the salad and top with capers.

Mix the oil, lemon juice, pepper, and salt then drizzle this over salad. Refrigerate for a few hours in a bowl covered with plastic wrap to allow the flavors to mingle.

Ingredients

lettuce leaves

2 cups canned tuna in water

1 red onion

2 tbsp capers

½ cup olive oil

1 lemon, juice squeezed

freshly ground pepper

salt

Tuna Salad

Serves **4**

Preparation

Tear the endive and lettuce into bite-sized pieces and set aside.

Thinly slice the cucumber and set aside.

Cut a small cross on the top of each tomato and plunge into boiling water for 30 seconds, then immerse in cold water. Using a small sharp knife remove the skins from the tomatoes, then slice the flesh crossways.

Place the endive, lettuce, cucumber, tomatoes, olives and onion in a serving bowl. Toss together until thoroughly combined.

Cut the cheese into ½-in cubes. Scatter over the salad in a serving bowl.

Place the remaining ingredients in a small bowl and whisk together with a fork until thickened.

Pour the dressing over the salad and serve immediately.

Feta Salad

Ingredients

½ small head curly endive

½ small head iceberg lettuce

1 small cucumber

4 large tomatoes

8–10 pitted green or black olives, halved

1 medium Spanish or red onion, sliced

4 oz feta cheese

5 tbsp olive oil

2 tbsp red wine vinegar

½ tsp freshly ground sea salt

¼ tsp freshly ground black pepper

½ tsp ready-made German mustard

1 tsp chopped fresh marjoram or oregano

Serves **4**

Preparation

Cut the meat into thin strips and place in a salad bowl.

Cut the onion in half, then thinly slice. Separate the half rings and add to the bowl.

Slice the gherkins and add to the bowl.

Crush the garlic and tear the basil leaves into pieces. Add to the bowl, then mix together all the salad ingredients thoroughly.

For the dressing: in a small bowl, whisk together the wine vinegar, oil and mustard with a fork until thickened. Stir in the chopped parsley and season to taste with salt and pepper.

Pour the dressing over the salad and toss to mix. Set aside for 1 hour to allow the flavors to mingle.

Arrange the lettuce leaves on individual serving plates and pile the salad on top. Garnish with capers before serving.

Mixed Meat Salad

Ingredients

1 lb 2 oz mixed cooked meats
such as pork, beef and chicken
1 onion
4 pickled gherkins
2 cloves garlic
a few leaves of fresh basil
2 tbsp white wine vinegar
4 tbsp olive oil
1 tsp mustard
1 tbsp chopped fresh parsley
salt and freshly ground black pepper
crisp lettuce leaves, to serve
capers, to garnish

salads

Serves **4**

Preparation

Combine all the ingredients—except the lettuce, chicken, avocado and lemon juice—in a food processor. Process the ingredients until smooth and well mixed. Chill in the refrigerator for at least 1 hour to allow the flavors to blend.

Shred the lettuce or tear into bite-sized pieces and arrange on 4 individual serving plates.

Cut the chicken into strips or cubes and arrange on top of the lettuce.

Toss the avocado slices or cubes in lemon juice before scattering over the chicken.

Spoon the dressing over the salad, and serve any remaining dressing separately.

Green Goddess Salad

Ingredients

8 anchovy fillets, soaked in milk, rinsed and dried

1 spring onion, chopped

2 tbsp chopped fresh tarragon

3 tbsp chopped fresh chives

4 tbsp chopped fresh parsley

1 cup prepared mayonnaise

½ cup plain yogurt

2 tbsp tarragon vinegar

a pinch of sugar and cayenne pepper

1 avocado, peeled and sliced or cubed

1 large head lettuce

1 lb cooked chicken

1 tbsp lemon juice

Tip

The dressing can be prepared in advance and kept in the refrigerator for a day or two.

Serves **6**

Preparation

Place frozen artichoke hearts (if using), in a large microwave-proof casserole dish and cover. Heat in a microwave oven on high for 3–4 minutes, or until slightly warm.

Stir in the remaining ingredients, except the dressing and salad leaves, and heat on high for 2 minutes to warm through.

Place the dressing ingredients in a small bowl and whisk together with a fork until thickened. Pour over the warm salad and toss to coat.

Arrange the radicchio and endive leaves on individual serving plates. Pile the salad on top. Spoon over any excess dressing and serve immediately.

Place frozen artichoke hearts on plates (if using).

Salade **de Legumes**

Ingredients

9–10 oz frozen or canned artichoke hearts

1 red onion, chopped or 4 spring onions, thinly sliced

1 clove garlic, crushed

1 green pepper, seeded and chopped

1 tsp chopped fresh basil

1 tsp chopped fresh thyme

2 tsp chopped fresh parsley

1 lb canned haricot, white kidney or butter beans, rinsed and drained

For the dressing

1 clove garlic

2 tbsp white wine

1 tbsp red wine vinegar

5 tbsp olive oil

1 onion, finely sliced

salt and freshly ground black pepper

¼ tsp salt

Tip

Mix the dressing into the warm ingredients immediately to bring out their flavours.

Serves **4–6**

Preparation

Tear the radicchio and romaine lettuce leaves into bite-sized pieces. Pull apart the watercress, but keep the leaves whole. If using watercress, remove any thick stems and yellow leaves. Toss all the salad leaves together in a large salad bowl.

Add the tomatoes, chicken, cheese, gherkins and walnuts to the salad bowl and lightly toss to mix.

Place the oils and wine vinegar in a small bowl and whisk with a fork until thickened. Fold in the fromage frais and the tarragon leaves. Whisk thoroughly, then season to taste with salt and pepper.

Drizzle some of the dressing over the salad before serving. Serve the salad with the remainder of the dressing in a small jug.

Ingredients

1 head radicchio leaves, separated
1 head romaine lettuce
1 bunch watercress
4 oz cherry tomatoes, halved and cored
4 chicken breasts, cooked, skinned and thinly sliced
4 oz Bresse blue, or other blue cheese, cut into small pieces
16 small pickled gherkins, thinly sliced
2 oz walnut halves
2 tbsp each vegetable and walnut oil, mixed
2 tbsp white wine vinegar
¾ cup fromage frais
2 tsp chopped fresh tarragon leaves
salt and freshly ground black pepper

Salade **Bresse**

Tip

If you want to prepare this salad in advance, do not add the dressing until the last minute, otherwise the leaves will go limp.

Serves **4**

Preparation

Place the oil and lemon juice in a bowl and season with salt and pepper. Mix together thoroughly.

Cut the avocados in half lengthways, then remove and discard the stones. Peel, then cut into neat slices.

Mix the avocado slices with the oil and lemon juice very carefully, taking care not to break them up.

Cut the apricots in half, then remove and discard the stones. If the apricots are large, cut in half again. Add to the avocados in the dressing.

In another bowl, mix together the yogurt, honey, lemon rind and parsley.

Divide the lettuce leaves between 4 individual serving plates and arrange the avocado and apricots on top in a sunflower design.

Spoon a little of the yogurt mixture over the salad, then sprinkle with sunflower seeds. Pour any remaining yogurt dressing into a small jug and serve separately.

Green and Gold Sunflower Salad

Ingredients

3 tbsp sunflower oil

1 tbsp lemon juice

2 large ripe avocado pears

8 ripe apricots

½ cup plain yogurt

2 tsp honey

grated rind of 1 lemon

2 tsp chopped fresh parsley

1 small head butter lettuce, separated into leaves

2 oz toasted sunflower seeds

salt and freshly ground black pepper

Serves **4–6**

Preparation

Break the watercress into small sprigs, discarding any yellow leaves. Set aside. Carefully remove the peel and center from the oranges using a small sharp knife. Catch any juice that spills in a small bowl.

Remove the fleshy segments from between the thin membranes inside the oranges. Squeeze any juice from the orange membranes into the bowl with the juice from the peel.

Arrange the watercress with the orange segments on a serving dish.

Place the remaining ingredients in the bowl with the reserved orange juice and whisk together with a fork until thickened.

Pour the salad dressing over the oranges and watercress just before serving to prevent the watercress from going limp.

Serving suggestion: Serve the salad on a bed of finely grated carrot.

Variations: Use grapefruit in place of oranges. Use chicory in place of watercress.

Watercress and Orange Salad

Ingredients

3 large bunches watercress

4 oranges

6 tbsp vegetable oil

juice and rind of 1 orange

a pinch of sugar

1 tsp lemon juice

salt and freshly ground black pepper

Serves **4**

Preparation

Slice the tomatoes and cucumber and place in a salad bowl.

Cut the peppers in half lengthways. Remove and discard the cores and seeds, then slice the flesh into thin strips. Add to the salad bowl.

Slice the onions and separate the rings. Add to the salad bowl.

Tear the lettuce leaves into pieces and add to the bowl. Toss the salad ingredients to mix.

For the dressing: in a small bowl, whisk together the oil, wine vinegar, 1 tablespoon water and chopped herbs with a fork until thickened. Season to taste with salt, pepper and a little sugar.

Pour the dressing over the salad and toss thoroughly to coat.

Garnish the salad with the hard-boiled egg slices and olives before serving.

Ingredients

5 tomatoes

1 cucumber

3 peppers

2–3 red onions

1 head lettuce, leaves separated

1 hard-boiled egg, sliced

stuffed olives, to garnish

For the dressing

3 tbsp olive oil

4 tbsp wine vinegar

1 tbsp chopped fresh parsley

1 tbsp chopped fresh chives

salt and freshly ground black pepper

sugar

Spanish Salad

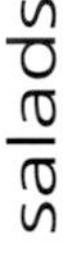

Serves **4**

Preparation

Tear the larger lettuce leaves into pieces and place all the lettuce in a salad bowl.

Trim the radishes. Thinly slice larger radishes and cut smaller radishes into quarters. Add to the salad bowl.

Cut the cucumber in half lengthways, remove the seeds and cut the flesh into slices about 2 in wide. Add to the salad bowl.

Cut half the olives in half and finely slice the remainder. Add the halved olives to the other salad ingredients.

For the dressing: press the cheese through a sieve into a small bowl. Whisk with the sour cream, oil and wine vinegar until smooth.

Add the sliced olives, pepper, sugar (to taste) and the chopped herbs to the dressing.

Spoon the dressing over the salad before serving.

Summer Salad
with Blue Cheese Cream

Ingredients

1 head lettuce, leaves separated

1 bunch radishes

½ cucumber

10 green stuffed olives

1 ¾ oz blue cheese

2 tbsp sour cream

3 tbsp olive oil

2 tbsp white wine vinegar

freshly ground black pepper

1 tbsp finely chopped fresh herbs

sugar

Tip

Use ripe Stilton or Roquefort for the dressing.

Serves **4**

Preparation

Trim the French beans and cut into shorter lengths. Cook in a pan of salted boiling water for about 3–4 minutes until just tender. Drain thoroughly and set aside.

For the dressing: in a bowl, whisk together the oil, wine vinegar, salt, pepper and sugar (to taste) with a fork until thickened.

Add the chopped herbs and onion to the dressing and mix well.

Mix the warm French beans with the drained canned beans in a serving dish. Pour over the dressing and toss thoroughly to coat.

Allow the salad to stand for at least 30 minutes before serving.

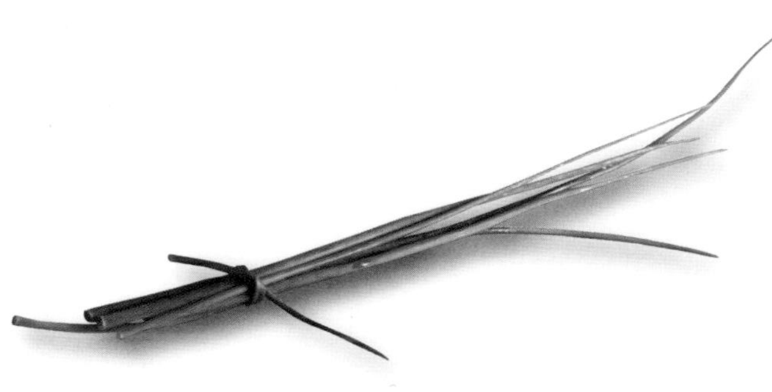

Ingredients

1 lb french beans

14 oz can red kidney beans, drained

14 oz can haricot beans, drained

For the dressing

3 tbsp salad oil

1–2 tbsp wine vinegar

salt and freshly ground black pepper

1 tbsp chopped mixed herbs

1 onion, finely chopped

sugar

Bean Salad

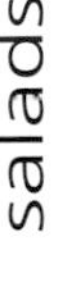

PASTA, RICE & POTATOES

Preparation

Wash, pat dry, and chop the basil, then grind with the parsley, garlic, and salt in a mortar with a pestle.

Add the Parmesan and grated goat cheese. Mix well. Add 1 tablespoon oil and stir until creamy or combine all ingredients with an electric mixer.

Cook pasta in salted water until al dente according to the instructions on the package. Drain in a sieve and place in a pre-heated bowl.

Toss the pasta and sauce and serve immediately.

Serving suggestion: Serve with extra grated Parmesan cheese.

Ingredients

For the sauce

1 bunch basil leaves

3–4 tbsp minced parsley

5 garlic cloves, peeled

1 tsp salt

4 tbsp grated Parmesan cheese

6 tbsp grated Pecorino cheese

10 tbsp olive oil

14 oz spaghetti

Spaghetti Genoese-style

Preparation

Peel and mince the onions and garlic. Heat the oil and sauté them.

Add the ground beef and brown for 5 minutes. Break up the meat into smaller pieces with a fork. Season with salt, pepper, and paprika.

Add the canned tomatoes and their liquid, and break up any lumps of meat with a spoon. Add the tomato paste and red wine or water, stir, and bring to a boil.

Cook for 10 minutes, then add the thyme and basil.

Add a little oil to boiling salted water. Cook the pasta until al dente according to instructions on the package. Drain in a colander.

Serve with Parmesan cheese if desired.

Spaghetti Bolognese

Ingredients

For the sauce

2 onions

1–2 cloves garlic

2 tbsp olive oil

8 oz ground beef and pork (half of each)

salt, freshly ground pepper

sweet paprika

14 oz canned tomatoes

5 tbsp tomato paste

½ cup red wine or water

1 tsp dried thyme

1 tsp chopped fresh basil

For the spaghetti

14 oz spaghetti

1 tbsp vegetable oil

grated Parmesan cheese

Serves **4**

Preparation

Rub a skillet with a clove of garlic. Peel and chop the onion. Heat oil in the pan and sauté onion. Add ground beef and brown. Add the tomato paste and simmer. Season with salt, pepper, rosemary, oregano, and thyme. Add the broth and simmer for a few minutes. Mix crème fraîche, milk, and Parmesan cheese.

Place layer of lasagna in a buttered baking dish. Cover with the meat sauce, and repeat, making alternate layers. The top layer should be meat sauce (the noodles should be completely covered). Dot with butter and top with cheese mixture. Place in the oven.

Oven

Conventional oven: 400–425 °F (preheated)

Fan-assisted oven: 175–400 °F (preheated)

Gas oven: Mark 4 (preheated)

Cooking time: around 35 minutes

Tip: Stir 4–5 skinned, chopped tomatoes into the sauce.

Serving suggestion: Tomato salad

Lasagne al Forno

Ingredients

1 garlic clove, peeled; 1 large onion

1 tbsp oil

½ cup ground beef; ½ cup ground pork

3 tbsp tomato paste

salt and freshly ground pepper

pinch of dried rosemary

pinch each of dried oregano and dried thyme

1 cup meat broth

⅔ cup crème fraîche

½ cup milk

3 tbsp grated Parmesan cheese

8 oz package lasagna; 3 tbsp butter

Serves **6**

Preparation

Cook the pasta in water with the oil and salt until al dente, according to the package instructions. Drain in a colander and keep warm.

Wash and dry the lemon, peel off a thin strip of rind and reserve. Grate the rest of the rind and reserve. Cut off the white parts, and divide the lemon into segments.

Cut the segments into small pieces, mix with the heavy cream and vodka. Add the strip of rind. Bring to a boil and cook for 5 minutes. Add the lemon juice. Return to a boil and cook for another 5 minutes. Season the sauce with salt, pepper, and sugar. Discard the piece of rind.

Mix the cooked pasta with the lemon sauce and grated Parmesan. Place on a serving platter and sprinkle with the grated lemon rind.

Ingredients

1 lb 5 oz fettuccini (tagliatelle),

1 tbsp vegetable oil, salt

For the sauce

1 untreated lemon

2 cups heavy cream

3–4 tbsp vodka

1 lemon, juice squeezed

salt, freshly ground pepper

sugar; 3 tbsp grated Parmesan cheese

Fettuccini with Lemon Sauce

Tip

Serve with lettuce leaves or serve the fettuccine with lemon sauce as a side-dish with chicken breast or Vienna schnitzel and mixed green salad

Preparation

Bring the pasta to a boil in salted water; add the oil, and cook according to the package instructions, then drain. Heat the butter, add the pasta, toss, and keep warm.

Peel the onion and garlic and mince it for the shellfish cooking liquid. Heat the oil and sauté the onion for 5 minutes, add the garlic and cook for 1 minute. Add the wine and bay leaf. Season with salt and pepper.

Add the mussels and cook for 5 minutes or until they open, stirring frequently. Dip tomatoes in boiling water for a few seconds, then plunge into cold water, remove skins and cores; cut in half, and dice.

Drain the bottled or canned mussels; defrost the shrimp. Add the tomatoes, clams, shrimp, mussels, and capers to the cooking liquid. Stir gently, bring to a boil and cook on low heat for 2 minutes.

Add pasta and parsley, toss lightly, and serve immediately.

Ingredients

14 oz fettuccine

1 tbsp vegetable oil

2–3 tbsp butter

For the shellfish cooking liquid

1 onion; 1 clove garlic

1 tbsp vegetable oil

½ cup white wine

12 oz fresh or frozen clams

about 2 cups tomatoes

about 1 cup mussels, fresh or canned

about ⅔ cup fresh or frozen shrimp

salt; freshly ground pepper

1 tbsp capers

chopped parsley

1 bayleaf

Fettuccine with Shellfish

Preparation

Cook fettuccini pasta in a large pot with boiling salted water until al dente. Drain. Stir in pesto sauce and 2 tablespoons of olive oil.

Sauté onion and garlic in 3 tablespoons olive oil in a large skillet until soft. Add green bell pepper, mushrooms and cook until soft, about 3 minutes. Stir in dry white wine, lemon juice, salt and pepper to taste, and bring to a boil. Add scallops and toss for 2 minutes. Take care not to overcook the scallops, as they will toughen when exposed to prolonged heat.

Toss the pesto covered pasta with the scallop sauce. Sprinkle with grated Parmesan cheese. Serve immediately.

Pasta with Pesto and Scallops

Ingredients

16 oz dry fettucine pasta

¼ cup pesto

2 tbsp olive oil

3 tbsp olive oil

½ onion, chopped

2 cloves garlic, minced

1 green bell pepper, thinly sliced

2 tbsp grated Parmesan cheese

½ cup fresh sliced mushrooms

2 tbsp dry white wine

ground black pepper

2 tbsp lemon juice

1 pound scallops

salt

pasta, rice & potatoes

Serves **3**

Preparation

Bring the pasta to a boil in boiling salted water. Add the oil, and cook according to the package instructions. Drain well.

Heat the butter, add the pasta, and toss. Place the pasta in a bowl and keep it warm.

Peel and chop the garlic. Clean the mushrooms, rinse if necessary, and slice. Wash, dry, and mince the parsley. Drain the mussels, reserving the liquid.

Heat the butter or margarine in a saucepan and sauté the garlic. Add the mushrooms and parsley, and sauté for 5 minutes. Add 1 tablespoon of the mussel liquid, cover the pot, and simmer for 10 minutes. Add the mussels and heat through. Season with salt, pepper, and onion powder. Spoon the mixture over the pasta and serve immediately.

Fettuccine with Mussels

Ingredients

8 oz fettuccini (tagliatelle)
1 tbsp vegetable oil
2 tbsp butter
1–2 cloves garlic
2 cups mushrooms
1 bunch parsley
4 cups canned mussels (without shell)
4 tbsp butter or margarine
onion powder
pepper
salt

Serves **3–4**

Preparation

Pre-cook spaghetti in boiling water, refresh in cold water, stir with half the oil and set aside.

Heat the remaining oil in a large cooking pot over high heat. Add the onion, garlic and cook for one minute

Add vongoles (clams), white wine, salt and pepper.

When all vongoles (clams) have opened, add spaghetti and oregano; cook for another 2 minutes and serve.

Ingredients

10 oz spaghetti

3 tbsp virgin olive oil

1 onion, chopped very finely

2 cloves garlic, finely chopped

1 lb vongoles (clams) cleaned

7 tbsp white wine

salt and pepper

1 tbsp fresh chopped oregano

Spaghetti Vongole

Serves **4–6**

Preparation

Cook pasta in a large pot of boiling salted water until al dente.

Pour cream into large skillet meanwhile. Cook over medium heat, stirring constantly, until just about boiling. Reduce heat and add herbs, salt, peppers, onions, and parsley. Simmer 7 to 8 minutes or until thickened.

Stir in seafood, cooking until shrimp is no longer transparent. Stir in cheeses, blending well.

Drain pasta. Serve sauce over noodles.

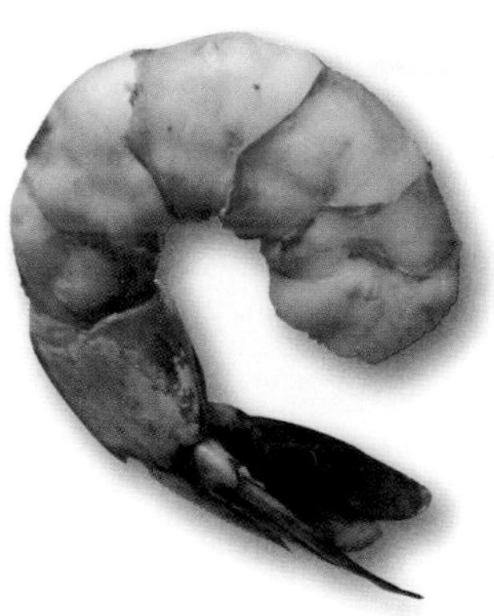

Cajun Seafood Pasta

Ingredients

2 cups heavy whipping cream

1 tbsp chopped fresh basil

1 tbsp chopped fresh thyme

1 ½ tsp crushed red pepper flakes

2 tsp ground black pepper

1 tsp ground white pepper

2 tsp salt

1 cup chopped green onions

1 cup chopped parsley

½ lb shrimp, peeled and deveined

½ lb scallops

½ cup shredded Swiss cheese

½ cup grated Parmesan cheese

1 pound dry fettucine pasta

pasta, rice & potatoes

Preparation

Heat the oil in a deep skillet. Peel and chop the onion and garlic, then sauté. Add the spinach (without thawing) and a little water. Simmer for 15 minutes, covered. Season with salt, pepper, and grated nutmeg. Drain and spoon into greased ovenproof dish.

Melt the butter and mix with flour. Heat until golden-brown, stirring constantly. Add the milk and heavy cream, beating well with a whisk. Bring to a boil and cook for 2 minutes. Season with salt and pepper.

Mix one-third of the sauce with half the Parmesan cheese. Reserve the rest of cream sauce. Pour half of the cheese sauce over the spinach and use other half to fill the manicotti (preferably with a piping bag).

Place the filled manicotti on the spinach and pour over the remaining cream sauce. Sprinkle with the remaining Parmesan cheese. Dot with butter and place on the center rack of the oven.

Serving suggestion: Tomato salad

Ingredients

1 tbsp vegetable oil

1 onion

1 clove garlic

1 lb 5 oz deep-frozen leaf spinach

freshly ground pepper

salt

nutmeg

For the sauce

3 tbsp butter

3 tbsp all-purpose flour

1 ¾ cups milk

½ cup heavy cream

1 cup grated Parmesan cheese

6 manicotti

Manicotti with Leaf Spinach

Oven

Conventional oven: 425 °F (preheated)

Fan-assisted oven: 400 °F (preheated)

Gas oven: Mark 4–5 (preheated)

Baking time: 20–30 minutes

Preparation

Toast the grated coconut in a dry skillet until golden, then add the water. Cover and leave to cool. Transfer the coconut to a paper towel and squeeze out the water. Reserve the squeezed liquid.

Peel and mince the onion and garlic, fry in the oil, add the curry powder, and continue cooking for 2 minutes, then add the coconut liquid. Set aside.

Boil the rice in the chicken broth for about 10 minutes; dice the crabsticks and ginger and add them to the broth.

Reheat the rice and arrange on a serving platter. Add salt and pepper to taste. Slice the hardboiled eggs. Skin, deseed, and dice the tomatoes. Garnish the rice with the tomato flesh.

Serving suggestion: Mixed leaf salad.

Basmati Rice with Crabsticks and Ginger

Ingredients

⅔ cup unsweetened shredded coconut
1 ¾ cups water
1 large onion
1 clove garlic
3 tbsp vegetable oil
2 tsp curry powder
1 ⅓ cups basmati rice
3 cups chicken broth
freshly ground pepper
3 oz candied ginger
2 hardboiled eggs
2 tomatoes
8 crabsticks
salt

Tip

Add 2⁄3 cup cooked, peeled shrimp to the crabsticks

Preparation

Peel and mince the onions. Heat the oil and fry the minced onions in a saucepan. Scald the tomatoes in boiling water (don't let them cook), and rinse them in cold water. Skin them, discard the core, and cut into quarters.

Deseed and dice, then and add the flesh to the onions. Wash the rice, add to the mixture, and sauté, stirring until the rice is glazed. Add half the broth and half the tomato juice; season with salt, pepper, and oregano. Bring to a boil and then simmer gently. When the liquid has evaporated add the rest of the tomato juice and the broth, one tablespoon at a time.

Cook on low heat for around 25 minutes until the risotto has a creamy consistency.

Stir the cheese into the rice and reheat. Season with salt and pepper to taste.

Ingredients

2 onions

5 tbsp oil

3 tomatoes

1 cup round-grain rice

2 cups tomato juice

1 cup vegetable broth

freshly ground pepper

oregano leaves

3 tbsp grated yellow cheese

salt

Risotto Pomodori

Tip

Serve Risotto Pomodori with stir-fried meat or fish goujons or with a mixed salad for a vegetarian meal.

Preparation

Wash and strain the beansprouts and bamboo shoots. Wash the leeks and slice them into rings.

Heat the sesame oil in a wok. Fry the leek rings, beansprouts, and bamboo shoots. Add the rice and shrimp, then sauté (the rice may change color). Season with salt, pepper, katjap, and sambal.

Rinse the chives, pat dry and cut into small rings. Beat the eggs with the chives, pour over the rice and let it curd vigorously.

Added ingredient:

Krupuk (Indonesian fish or seafood chips)

If unavailable, add Chinese shrimp crackers. The katjap can be replaced by a mixture of soy sauce and Thai or Vietnamese fish sauce.

Indonesian Fried Rice

Ingredients

1 ¾ cups beansprouts

1 ½ cups fresh or canned bamboo sprouts

1 small leek

4 tbsp sesame oil

1 ¾ cups long-grain rice, cooked

1 cup bay shrimp

freshly ground pepper

katjap (Indonesian soy sauce)

sambal oelek (Indonesian hot spice)

1 bunch chives

4 eggs

salt

Preparation

Peel and grate the onion. Melt the butter and fry the onion, add the rice, and fry until glazed, stirring frequently.

Mix the crème fraîche and dried herbs with enough broth to make 2 cups. Add to the rice, bring to a boil, and leave to simmer for around 20 minutes.

Trim the green parts from the green onions by around 4–6 inches, rinse and slice thinly. Clean the chanterelles or oyster mushrooms, wash if necessary, and halve or quarter the larger mushrooms. Cut into strips.

Melt the butter, fry the green onions, add all the mushrooms, and season to taste. Add the peas, cover the pan, and stew for 5–7 minutes.

Stir in the boiled rice and parsley. Season to taste before serving.

Ingredients

1 onion
1 tbsp butter
1 cup long-grain rice
½ cup crème fraîche
1 tsp dried mixed herbs
1 ¾ cups vegetable broth

1 bunch green onions (scallions)
2 cups chanterelles or oyster mushrooms
1 tbsp butter; salt
freshly ground pepper
1 ¾ cups frozen peas
1–2 tbsp minced parsley

Wild Mushroom **Risotto**

Tip

Serve the mushroom risotto with a beef, game, or chicken stew

Preparation

Bring a pot of salted water to a boil, add the rice and stir well. Bring this to a rolling boil for about 20 minutes. Sieve the rice, rinse it in cold water and let it strain well. Keep the rice warm.

Peel and chop the onions, fry in melted fat until they become translucent.

Wash the bell pepper, remove the seeds and white parts, chop into pieces, and add it to the onions. Season with salt and pepper. Cover the pot and simmer the contents for about 10 minutes.

Add the corn, blending in well. Bring back to a boil and cook for 5 minutes. Season again with salt and pepper. Mix everything into the rice.

Mexican Rice

Ingredients

8 cups salted water

1 cup pre-cooked long-grain rice

1 onion

2 tbsp unsalted butter or margarine

1 large red bell pepper

freshly ground pepper

6 tbsp canned corn

salt

Preparation

Strain the bamboo shoots in a colander and slice them into matchstick strips. Peel and wash the carrots and cut them into matchstick strips. Slice the leek in half, wash, and cut into rings. Wash the mushrooms, strain and cut into matchstick strips.

Cut the pepper in half and remove the stem, pits, and ribs. Wash and cut into strips. Shred, wash and drain the cabbage. Peel and mince the garlic.

Coat a wok with oil; heat the oil and fry the garlic. Beat the eggs and add them gradually to the wok with the rice. Stir-fry for about 1 minute. Add the vegetable strips and beansprouts and fry for about 3 minutes.

Season the dish with ketjap or soy sauce, salt, sugar, pepper, and monosodium glutamate (optional). Continue stir-frying for about 1 minute and serve hot.

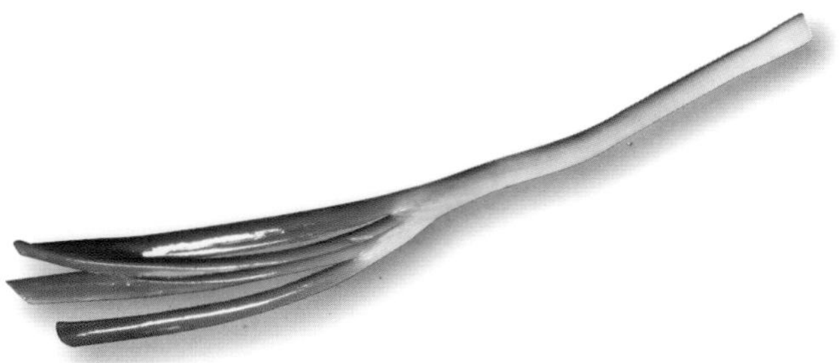

Oriental Fried Rice

Ingredients

2 oz can bamboo shoots
4 carrots
3 leeks
2 fresh Chinese mushrooms (shiitake)
1 red bell pepper
1 small Chinese (Napa) cabbage
1 clove garlic
6 tbsp oil

1–2 eggs
2 cups boiled rice
2 oz fresh beansprouts
3 tbsp ketjap (Indonesian soy sauce) or soy sauce
1 tsp salt
1 ⅓ tbsp sugar
½ tsp pepper
1 tsp monosodium glutamate (optional)

Serves **4**

Preparation

Heat the oil in a skillet on medium heat. Sauté the minced onion, finely chopped garlic and chili pepper for 2 minutes in the hot oil. Add the rice, together with half of the wine, and reduce while stirring with a wooden spoon until nearly all the wine has evaporated. Stir the mussels into the rice and add the rest of the wine. Add the herbs and simmer with the lid on the saucepan until both rice and mussels are tender. To prevent the rice from sticking to the bottom of the pan, you must stir the dish continually.

Sprinkle with parmesan cheese just before serving.

Mussel Risotto

Ingredients

1 cup olive oil

1 onion, minced

1 red chili pepper, chopped fine

10 oz risotto rice

2 ½ cups dry white wine

2 lbs ready-to-cook mussels

1 tbsp fresh herbes de Provence

(thyme, marjoram and rosemary), chopped fine

2 tbsp grated Parmesan cheese

Preparation

Rinse the pork, pat dry, and cut into cubes. Scald the tomatoes in boiling water (do not let them cook), and rinse them in cold water. Skin them, remove the cores and cut into quarters. Wash the peppers and cut them into pieces. Peel and slice the onions.

Dice the bacon and sauté in melted fat with the pork, allowing them to brown. Add the onions and peppers and continue to fry for about 10 minutes. Season with salt, pepper, tomato paste, tabasco, sweet paprika powder, and cayenne pepper. Add the basil and lovage leaves.

Add the beef broth and simmer for about 15 minutes. Add the tomatoes, rice, and water and cook for another 30 minutes.

Pork and Rice Medley

Ingredients

1 lb lean pork fillet

1 ¼ lb tomatoes

2 large bell peppers; 1 red, 1 green

2 large onions

3 slices bacon

4 tsp unsalted butter or margarine; salt

freshly ground pepper

2 tbsp tomato paste

tabasco; sweet paprika powder

cayenne pepper

chopped basil leaves

a few lovage leaves

1 cup meat broth

1 cup long-grain rice

2 cups water

Serves **6–8**

Preparation

Wash the potatoes and pat them dry. Cut them into thin slices. Beat the eggs in a bowl. Heat the oil in a frying pan and add the potatoes and onion. Season with salt and cover the pan.

Fry the potatoes gently. Shake the pan regularly to avoid sticking. Take the potatoes out once they are done, but not crispy, and add to the beaten eggs. Mix everything well so that the potatoes are completely covered in egg. Add salt. Heat approximately 1 tablespoon of the remaining oil.

Put the egg and potato mixture back in the pan and fry for a few minutes until one side is golden brown. Get ready a plate that is a little larger than the pan. Let the omelet slide carefully onto the plate with the golden brown side facing down. Slide back into the pan with the golden brown side facing up.

Fry the omelet until it is firm; it should be about 2 inches thick.

Cut into squares and serve as tapas.

Potato Omelet

Ingredients

2 ¼ lbs potatoes, peeled

1 small onion, peeled and roughly chopped (to taste)

1 ¼ cup olive oil

5 eggs, beaten

salt

Serves **4**

Preparation

Slice the sausages and potatoes. Make one cut lengthwise into the center of the leek, wash, and slice it into rings. Beat the eggs and heavy cream.

Wash, pat dry, and coarsely chop the parsley. Stir the parsley into the egg mixture. Sauté the potatoes and sausage in oil. Add the leeks and stir-fry for a few more minutes.

Season with salt and pepper. Pour the egg mixture into the pan and cook on low heat until it sets. Sprinkle with grated cheese and place under a preheated broiler until the cheese melts and bubbles.

Serve with lettuce, gherkins, and onions or sweet pickles.

Potatoes Speedy Gonzales

Ingredients

4 frying sausage links (around 3 oz each)

1 lb 5 oz boiled potatoes

1 large leek

4 medium eggs

1 cup heavy cream

1 bunch parsley

3 tbsp vegetable oil

1 ¾ cups grated mild yellow cheese

freshly ground pepper

salt

Serves **1**

Preparation

Peel the potatoes and cut into cubes.

Season the potato cubes with salt, then heat the oil in a pan and cook the potatoes for 10 minutes, turning frequently to cook evenly.

Add the onion, ginger, garlic and curry powder to the potatoes.

Add about ¼ cup water to the pan and stir to mix. Cover and cook for 10–12 minutes, stirring occasionally, until the potatoes are cooked and tender.

Taste and adjust the seasoning and serve immediately, sprinkled with sesame seeds.

Curried Potatoes

Ingredients

9 oz potatoes

2 tbsp vegetable oil

1 onion, thinly sliced

½ in piece fresh root ginger, finely chopped

1 clove garlic, crushed

salt

1 ½ tsp curry powder

1–2 tbsp sesame seeds

Tip

Curry paste can be used in place of curry powder.

VEGETABLES

Preparation

Cut bell peppers in half lengthwise and cut or pull out the stems and seeds, along with the white ribs. Place them on a dry cookie sheet in the oven.

Roast the peppers until the skins blister and begin to blacken. Cover briefly with a damp paper towel.

Peel off the skins and slice the flesh into strips. Wash the zucchini, trim the ends, and cut into slices. Peel and chop the garlic. Wash the basil, pat dry, pick off and chop the leaves. Slice the mozzarella. Lightly grease a jelly-roll pan, add bell pepper, mozzarella, zucchini, and black olives. Season with salt and pepper. Mix the oil with garlic and basil and pour the mixture over the vegetables. Place in the oven.

Italian Vegetable Bake

Ingredients

2 yellow bell peppers; 2 red bell peppers

4 medium zucchini; 1 clove garlic

1 bunch basil; 7 oz mozzarella

4 tbsp black olives, pitted

salt; freshly ground pepper

6 tbsp soya oil

Oven

Conventional oven: 400 °F (preheated)

Fan-assisted oven: 375 °F (preheated)

Gas oven: Mark 3–4 (preheated)

Baking time: 25–30 minutes

Tip

Serve with French bread and chianti.

vegetables

Serves **8**

Preparation

Slice the olives, chop the anchovies and onion, and slice the cheese thinly. Mix all ingredients with all but 2 tbsp of the oil and salt.

Layer the mixture with the broccoli in a casserole or Dutch oven. The top layer should be broccoli. Drizzle with remaining oil. Add enough red wine to cover the vegetables. Cover the pot and transfer it to the oven. Cook on low heat for 1 ½ hours or until all wine has been absorbed.

Sicilian Broccoli

Ingredients

2 tbsp pitted black olives

8 anchovy fillets

1 small onion, peeled

2 oz mature half–fat cheese

1 cup olive oil

10 cups broccoli flowerets

around 2 cups dry red wine

salt

Preparation

Wash eggplants. Cut lengthwise into finger-thick slices, keeping the slices still attached at one end. Sprinkle the cut sides with salt, and drain in a sieve for 30 minutes. Rinse under cold running water. Pat dry with paper towel and arrange in a greased oven dish.

Drop the tomatoes briefly in boiling water (do not cook), then plunge into cold water. Skin, core, and slice them.

Peel and chop the garlic. Drain the mozzarella and cut into thin slices. Insert alternate slices of tomato, mozzarella, and salami into the eggplants. Sprinkle with garlic, drizzle with oil, and place in the oven. Cover with nonstick baking paper.

Sprinkle with parsley before serving.

Baked **Eggplants**

Ingredients

4 medium eggplants

salt; 8 tomatoes; 6 garlic cloves

7 oz mozzarella; 8 slices salami

6 tbsp olive oil; minced parsley

Oven

Conventional oven: 400 °F (preheated)

Fan-assisted oven: 375 °F (preheated)

Gas oven: Mark 3–4 (preheated)

Baking time: around 50 minutes

Preparation

Wash the eggplant, trim the ends, and dice. Sprinkle with salt and steep for 10 minutes. Rinse under cold running water and drain. Peel and chop the onion. Slice the bell peppers in half lengthwise and remove stems and seeds, along with the white ribs. Wash and cut into strips. Wash the zucchini, trim the ends, and cut into thin slices. Peel and chop the garlic.

Heat the oil in a flameproof casserole or Dutch oven, and cook the vegetables for 5 minutes, stirring constantly. Add the wine and vinegar, season with salt, pepper, sugar, and herbs.

Cover the pot and simmer the vegetables for 15–20 minutes.

Mix the tomato paste with the tomato juice, add to vegetables. Add the liquid seasoning, bring back to a boil, and transfer to a serving bowl.

Ingredients

1 small eggplant; 1 tbsp salt

1 medium onion

1 small red bell pepper

1 small green bell pepper

1 small zucchini

1 garlic clove; 2 tbsp olive oil

2–3 tbsp white wine

2–3 tbsp wine vinegar

freshly ground pepper

chopped basil

chopped oregano

1 tbsp tomato paste

½ cup tomato juice liquid seasoning

sugar

salt

Italian Eggplant and Pepper Stew

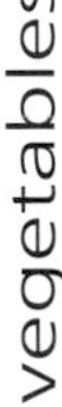

Serves **1**

Preparation

Peel or trim the vegetables, then cut into small pieces.

Place the prepared vegetables in a shallow pan, add a little water and cover. Cook for about 10 minutes until tender, stirring occasionally.

Melt the butter in a pan, add the lemon juice, rind and salt and pepper (to taste), then pour on the cream. Beat vigorously.

Drain and serve the vegetables on a warm plate, sprinkle with the chopped herbs and pour over the sauce. Serve immediately.

Mixed Vegetables with Lemon Butter

Ingredients

1 cup mixed vegetables such as carrots, sugar-snap peas, kohlrabi and celeriac (Knob celery)

2 tbsp butter

1 tsp lemon juice

rind of ½ lemon

salt and freshly ground black pepper

2–3 tbsp heavy cream

1 tbsp chopped fresh chervil or chives

vegetables

Serves **1**

Preparation

Hollow out each tomato and season with salt, pepper and thyme to taste.

Slice the sheep cheese and fill each tomato with a small slice of cheese.

Slice the olives in half and close each tomato with a lid of a half olive.

Cut both the eggplant and zucchini in half lengthwise.

Cut both vegetables into slices about ¾ in thick.

In a bowl, season the oil with salt and pepper and stir in the oregano and lemon juice. Add the vegetables, stir to mix and leave to marinate for 10 minutes.

Cut the cucumber into slices about 1 ¼ in thick.

Hollow out and discard the center and seeds with a small spoon and season the cucumber with salt and pepper.

Melt the butter in a pan and cook the mushrooms with salt and pepper (to taste) for 5 minutes. Sprinkle with chopped mint or parsley.

Stuff the cucumber slices with the mushrooms.

Press the tomatoes, eggplant, zucchini and cucumber slices alternately onto 2 kabob skewers, then brush the kabobs with the eggplant and zucchini marinade.

Place on a grill rack and cook under a preheated grill for about 10 minutes, turning the kabobs frequently to cook them evenly. Serve hot.

Ingredients

4 cherry tomatoes
salt and freshly ground black pepper
dried thyme
2 tbsp sheep cheese
2 pitted olives
½ small eggplant,
weighing about 3 ½ oz
½ small zucchini, weighing about 2 oz

2 tbsp olive oil
dried oregano, to taste
a dash of lemon juice
½ small cucumber, weighing about 7 oz
2 tsp fresh chopped mint or parsley
2 oz mushrooms, about
the same diameter as the cucumber
1 tbsp butter

Greek-Style **Vegetable Kabobs**

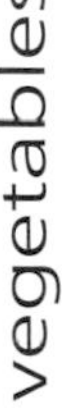

Serves **1**

Preparation

Heat the oil in a non-stick pan. Add the crumbled stock cube, onion, apple and carrot.

Cook gently for 5 minutes, stirring continuously.

In a bowl, mix the tomato purée with 5 tbsp water and add to the pan together with all the other ingredients except the beans and cream.

Stir well, cover and simmer for 2 minutes.

Add the beans, stir to mix, then transfer the mixture to an ovenproof casserole dish.

Cover and cook at 350 °F/Gas Mark 4 for about 30 minutes.

Add a little more water after 20 minutes, if necessary.

Top with a swirl of sour cream and serve immediately.

Savory Bean Pot

Ingredients

2 tsp vegetable oil

½ vegetable stock cube, crumbled

1 small onion, chopped

1 small apple, peeled and grated

1 small carrot, grated

1 tbsp tomato purée

2 tsp white wine vinegar

½ tsp dried mustard

a pinch of dried oregano

a pinch of ground cumin

½ tsp brown sugar

salt and freshly ground black pepper

½ cup cooked red kidney beans

a little sour cream

Tip

Canned kidney beans are ideal for this recipe and save you from having to cook the beans yourself at home.

Serves **1**

Preparation

Cut the zucchini in half lengthwise.

Using a teaspoon, remove the flesh leaving about a ¼ in zucchini shell.

Finely chop the flesh and set aside.

Heat the oil in a pan, add the onion and cook for a few minutes, stirring occasionally, until softened.

Add the carrot, zucchini flesh and spices. Cook, stirring frequently, for a further 5 minutes until softened.

Remove from the heat and stir in the creamed coconut.

Pile the mixture into the zucchini shells, making sure that it covers the exposed part of the flesh.

Place the zucchini halves in a greased ovenproof casserole dish and cook in a preheated oven at 375 °F/Gas Mark 5 for 30–45 minutes, until the zucchini shells are soft.

Serve immediately, garnished with fresh herb sprigs.

Stuffed Zucchini

Ingredients

1 medium zucchini

2 tsp olive oil

½ small onion, very finely chopped

2 tbsp carrot, grated

a pinch of paprika

¼ tsp cumin seeds

a pinch of turmeric

a pinch of asafoetida powder (optional)

2 tbsp creamed coconut, grated

fresh herb sprigs, to garnish

vegetables

Serves **2**

Preparation

Place the flour and salt in a bowl. Make a slight well in the centre and break in the egg. Using a wooden spoon, gradually incorporate the flour into the egg. Gradually add the milk or water and beat well to form a smooth batter. Set aside.

Heat the olive oil in a pan over medium heat, add the onion and garlic and cook for 2–3 minutes until softened but not browned, stirring frequently.

Add the peppers and zucchini and cook over low heat for about 10 minutes until softened, stirring frequently. Add the tomato, basil and tomato purée and cook for a further 5 minutes, stirring occasionally. Stir in the cheese, season to taste with salt and pepper and cook for a further 5 minutes, stirring occasionally. Set aside and keep warm.

To cook the pancakes: heat a little vegetable oil in a small frying pan. Pour in just enough batter to thinly coat the base of the pan. Cook for 1–2 minutes, until golden brown. Turn over the pancake and cook the second side until golden brown. Remove from the pan and keep the remaining batter warm while you cook.

Divide the vegetable mixture equally between each pancake and spread lightly with the back of a spoon. Roll up each filled pancake Swiss-roll style and place in an ovenproof serving dish.

Place in a preheated oven at 350 °F/Gas Mark 4 for 10 minutes, until hot. Serve, garnished with parsley sprigs.

Ingredients

1 oz all-purpose flour
a pinch of salt
1 small egg
5 tbsp milk or water
1 tbsp olive oil
1 small onion, finely chopped
1 clove garlic, crushed
1 small green pepper, seeded and diced
1 small red pepper, seeded and diced
1 tomato, skinned, seeded and chopped
1 small zucchini, diced
½ tsp chopped fresh basil
1 tbsp tomato purée
½ oz vegetarian cheese, crumbled
salt and freshly ground black pepper
vegetable oil, for frying
fresh parsley sprigs, to garnish

Pancakes Provençale

Serves **2**

Preparation

Heat the oil in a pan, add the rice and cook for 1 minute, stirring. Add the vegetable stock and season with salt and pepper.

Bring to a boil, then reduce the heat and simmer, uncovered, for 15–18 minutes, until all the liquid has been absorbed, stirring occasionally. Remove the pan from the heat and set aside.

Beat the eggs in a bowl, add the cream and curd cheese and mix well. Season to taste with salt, pepper and grated nutmeg.

Cook the root vegetables in a pan of boiling water for 8–10 minutes, or until tender. Drain, mash and set aside.

Blanch the mangetout for 3–4 minutes in a saucepan of boiling water, then remove, drain and mix with the mashed vegetables.

Finely chop the parsley. Grease an ovenproof dish, then fill with layers of the rice and mixed vegetables, ending with a layer of vegetables. Season each layer with salt and pepper and sprinkle with chopped parsley.

Pour the egg and cream mixture evenly over the top of the vegetables. Cover with cheese, dot with the butter flakes and bake in a preheated oven at 400 °F/ Gas Mark 6 for about 20 minutes, or until cooked and golden brown.

Garnish with fresh herb sprigs and serve immediately.

Ingredients

1 tbsp olive oil

3 oz long-grain rice

1 scant cup vegetable stock

salt and freshly ground black pepper

½ cup heavy double cream

5 tbsp low-fat curd cheese

grated nutmeg

2 eggs

13 oz prepared mixed root vegetables such as parsnips, swede, turnips and carrots, diced

½ cup mangetout, trimmed

1 bunch fresh flat-leaf parsley

3 tbsp grated Parmesan cheese

2 tbsp butter flakes

fresh herb sprigs, to garnish

Root Vegetable Risotto with Mangetout

Serves **2**

Preparation

Cook the broccoli in a saucepan of lightly salted, boiling water for about 5 minutes, until just tender. Drain well and set aside.

Heat the oil in a pan and cook the mushrooms and onions for 3 minutes, stirring. Remove the pan from the heat and stir in the broccoli.

Arrange the mixed vegetables in an oval ovenproof dish and season to taste with salt, pepper, turmeric and cumin.

Sprinkle over the sesame seeds and cheese.

For the sauce: mix the sesame seeds with the cream and crème fraîche and season with salt and pepper.

Pour the sauce over the vegetables. Bake in a preheated oven at 400 °F/ Gas Mark 6 for 20 minutes, until golden brown and bubbling. Serve hot.

Baked Broccoli

Ingredients

1 cup broccoli florets

2 tbsp vegetable oil

½ cup chestnut mushrooms, halved or sliced

¼ cup red onions, sliced

salt and freshly ground black pepper

ground turmeric

ground cumin

1 tbsp toasted sesame seeds

⅓ cup Emmenthal cheese, grated

For the sauce

2 tsp toasted sesame seeds

½ cup heavy double cream

2 tsp crème fraîche

salt and freshly ground black pepper

Serves **2**

Preparation

Fry the leeks, garlic, ginger and spices in a pan with oil until soft, stirring frequently. Add the mushrooms and cook over low heat until soft, stirring occasionally.

Add the grated coconut and cook gently until the coconut has completely dissolved, adding a little water if the mixture appears too dry.

Stir in the lemon juice and season with salt and pepper to taste. Serve hot, garnished with fresh herb sprigs.

Mushroom Curry

Ingredients

1 cup leeks, thinly sliced

2 cloves garlic, crushed

½ tsp grated root ginger

2 tsp curry powder

1 tsp garam masala

2 tbsp sunflower oil

2 ¼ cups mushroom

cut into quarters

½ cup creamed coconut, grated

1 tbsp lemon juice

salt and freshly ground black pepper

fresh herb sprigs, to garnish

vegetables

Serves **2**

Preparation

Cover the beans with water in a large microwave-proof bowl and cook in a microwave oven on high for 10 minutes. Leave to stand for 1 hour, then drain and discard the liquid.

Return the drained beans to the bowl and add the bay leaf, a little salt and pepper and enough fresh water to cover.

Cover the bowl with plastic wrap and pierce several times with the tip of a sharp knife. Cook the beans on medium for 1 hour, then allow to stand for 10 minutes before draining completely. Set aside.

Place the rice in another microwave-proof bowl with a little salt. Pour over 1 ¼ cups cold water. Cook the rice on high for 10 minutes. Leave to stand for 5 minutes, then drain and rinse in cold water. Set aside.

Place the butter or margarine in a microwave-proof bowl and melt on high for 30 seconds.

Add the pepper and mushrooms and stir well to coat them evenly before cooking on high for 2 minutes.

Stir the pepper and mushrooms, then add the cayenne pepper, nutmeg, cooked rice and beans.

Mix well, then cook on high for 3 minutes, stirring once during the cooking time.

Stir in the tomatoes and spring onions and cook on high for a further 1 minute before serving. Garnish with the chopped parsley.

Ingredients

⅓ cup dried red kidney beans
1 bay leaf
salt and freshly ground black pepper
⅓ cup long-grain brown or white rice
4 tsp butter or vegetable margarine
1 green pepper, seeded and cut into thin strips
¼ cup mushrooms, sliced
a pinch of cayenne pepper
a pinch of ground nutmeg
2 tomatoes, skinned, seeded and cut into strips
2 spring onions, chopped
1 tbsp chopped fresh parsley, to garnish

Red Bean **Creole**

Tip

Use a 6 oz can of beans, drained and omit Steps 1–3 instead of cooking your own beans.

vegetables

Serves **6**

Preparation

Break the cauliflower and broccoli into small florets and steam over a saucepan of boiling water for about 7–10 minutes, just until tender.

Melt the margarine in a pan, remove from the heat and gradually add the flour. Stir to form a roux, then add the milk gradually, blending well to ensure a smooth consistency.

Return the pan to the heat and stir until the sauce thickens and comes to a boil. Remove from the heat.

Cool a little, then add the cheese and egg yolk. Stir well and add the nutmeg. In a bowl, whisk the egg white until stiff, then fold carefully into the sauce.

Place the steamed vegetables into 6 small buttered ramekin dishes and season with salt and pepper.

Divide the sauce evenly between the dishes and bake immediately in a preheated oven at 375 °F/Gas Mark 5 for about 35 minutes, until puffed and golden. Serve at once.

Cauliflower and Broccoli **Souflettes**

Ingredients

1 ⅔ cup cauliflower

1 ⅔ cup broccoli

3 tbsp vegetable margarine

3 tbsp brown rice flour

2 cups milk

1 large egg, separated

a good pinch of ground nutmeg

salt and freshly ground black pepper

3 tbsp Cheddar cheese, grated

Serves **4**

Preparation

Cut the Chinese cabbage into four pieces and rinse thoroughly. Cook in a saucepan of salted boiling water for about 6 minutes.

Drain the cabbage, then place in a greased ovenproof dish.

Lay the mushroom slices over the cabbage and season to taste with salt and pepper.

In a bowl, mix the crème fraîche and yogurt together, beat in the eggs and season with salt and pepper.

Add grated nutmeg and curry powder, stir well, then pour the sauce over the mushrooms.

Sprinkle with the grated cheese and cook in a preheated oven at 400° F/ Gas Mark 6 for about 30 minutes, until golden brown. Serve hot.

Chinese Cabbage Gratin

Ingredients

3 cups Chinese cabbage
1 cup mushrooms, sliced
salt and freshly ground black pepper
⅔ cup crème fraîche
⅔ cup full fat plain yogurt
2 medium eggs
grated nutmeg, to taste
curry powder, to taste
½ cup mature Gouda cheese, grated

vegetables

Serves **4–6**

Preparation

Melt the butter in a pan, add the onion and cook until softened, stirring occasionally.

Drain the mushrooms, finely chop, then add to the pan. Cook for about 5 minutes, stirring occasionally.

Add the Cognac and 1 clove garlic. Increase the heat and cook until the juices in the pan are reduced, stirring frequently.

Stir in the parsley, remove the pan from the heat and set aside to cool.

In a bowl, mix the flour with the milk and cream, then stir in the mushroom mixture, shallots and peppercorns.

Mold the mixture together to create dumplings.

Cook the dumplings in a saucepan of salted, boiling water for 10–15 minutes. Drain well and set aside to cool.

Wash the spinach and cook in a saucepan with the olive oil until wilted without adding any water. Drain well and squeeze out any excess water. Chop the cooked spinach.

Add the remaining garlic and season with salt and pepper to taste.

Allow the spinach to cool, then mix with the quark and crème fraîche.

Serve the dumplings with the creamed spinach. Garnish with fresh herb sprigs.

Ingredients

2 tbsp butter
2 onions, thinly sliced
8 oz can mushrooms
1 tbsp Cognac
2 cloves garlic, thinly sliced
6 tbsp chopped fresh parsley
¾ cup all–purpose plain flour
about 1 cup milk
½ cup heavy cream
2 tbsp finely chopped shallots
1 tbsp green peppercorns
1 ⅓ cup fresh spinach leaves
1 tbsp olive oil
salt and freshly ground black pepper
1 ¼ cup quark (low-fat curd or cottage cheese)
⅔ cup crème fraîche
fresh herb sprigs, to garnish

Mushroom Dumplings with Creamed Spinach

Serves **2–4**

Preparation

Drain the quark thoroughly. In a bowl, mix the quark with the flour, salt, pepper, nutmeg and prepared vegetables.

Mix the wheat grains and pearl barley with the sunflower seeds and add to the quark mixture. Mix well.

Heat the margarine in a frying pan, then add the grain mixture. Spread out over the base of the pan and fry for about 5 minutes until it has formed a crust, then turn and fry the other side until crispy.

Break apart with 2 forks and fry the pieces for a further 2 minutes. Sprinkle with the grated cheese to serve.

Mixed Grain **Patties**

Ingredients

1 ⅔ cup quark (low-fat curd or cottage cheese)

1 cup plain wholemeal flour

grated nutmeg, to taste

1 bunch spring onions, finely sliced

freshly ground black pepper, to taste

1 tsp salt

1 bulb fennel, sliced

⅔ cup wheat grains, cooked

⅔ cup pearl barley, cooked

4 tbsp sunflower seeds

about 4 tbsp vegetable margarine

½ cup Emmenthal cheese, grated

Serves **4**

Preparation

Wash the lentils thoroughly under cold running water, then drain well. Place the lentils in a bowl, cover with water and leave to soak overnight.

Heat the oil in a pan, add the garlic and cook until softened. Add the prepared vegetables and cook briefly, stirring.

Stir in the tomato purée and stock, then bring to a boil.

Drain the lentils thoroughly, add to the pan and stir well. Cover and simmer for 30–40 minutes until the vegetables and lentils are almost cooked and tender, stirring occasionally.

Stir in the wine vinegar and thyme. Season with salt, pepper and cayenne, then stir in the honey. Continue cooking over a moderate heat for a further 10–15 minutes, stirring occasionally.

Chop the chives finely, leaving a few whole for garnishing.

Once the dish is cooked, adjust the seasoning and serve sprinkled with chopped chives.

Garnish with slices of leek and whole chives.

Ingredients

2 cups red lentils

2 tbsp olive oil

2 cloves garlic, crushed

1 onion, cut into small chunks

1 carrot, cut into small chunks

1 leek, cut into small chunks

1 stick celery, cut into small chunks

2–3 tbsp tomato purée

2 ½ cups vegetable stock

2 tbsp white wine vinegar

1 sprig fresh thyme

salt and freshly ground black pepper

a pinch of cayenne pepper

2 tbsp honey

1 bunch fresh chives

slices leek, to garnish

Red Lentils with Vegetables

MEAT & POULTRY

Preparation

Melt half the butter in a large frying pan. When sizzling, add fillet and cook over medium heat for 10 minutes, turning to brown and seal all sides. Remove meat from pan and set aside to cool completely.

Melt remaining butter in frying pan and cook onion for 5 minutes or until soft.

Add mushrooms and cook, stirring, for 15 minutes or until mushrooms give up all their juices. Season to taste with black pepper and nutmeg, stir in parsley and set aside to cool completely.

Roll out pastry to a length 4 inches longer than the meat and wide enough to wrap around the fillet. Spread half the mushroom mixture down the center of pastry and place fillet on top. Spread remaining mushroom mixture on top of fillet. Cut out the corners of pastry.

Brush pastry edges with egg. Wrap pastry around fillet like a parcel, tucking in ends. Place the pastry-wrapped fillet seam side down on a lightly greased baking sheet and freeze for 10 minutes.

Roll out remaining pastry to 4x12 in length and cut into strips ½ in wide. Remove fillet from freezer and brush pastry all over with egg. Arrange 5 pastry strips diagonally over pastry parcel, then arrange remaining strips diagonally in the opposite direction. Brush top of strips only with egg and bake 30 minutes for medium-rare beef. Place on a warmed serving platter and set aside to rest in a warm place for 10 minutes.

To make sauce: place wine in a small saucepan and cook over medium heat until reduced by half. Add thyme, parsley and black pepper to taste. Remove pan from heat and quickly whisk in one piece of butter at a time, ensuring that each piece is completely whisked in and melted before adding the next. Whisk in cornflour mixture and cook over medium heat, stirring until sauce thickens. Serve with sliced beef.

Oven

Conventional oven: 425 °F

Gas oven: Mark 7

Beef Fillet Wrapped in Pastry

Ingredients

¼ cup butter

2 lb fillet steak, trimmed of fat

1 onion, chopped

12 oz button mushrooms, finely chopped

freshly ground black pepper

pinch ground nutmeg

1 tbsp chopped fresh parsley

1 lb prepared puff pastry

1 egg, lightly beaten

Red wine sauce

1 cup red wine

1 tsp finely chopped fresh thyme or ¼ tsp dried thyme

1 tsp finely chopped fresh parsley

¼ cup butter, cut into small pieces

2 tsp cornstarch blended with 1 tbsp water

Preparation

Rinse the meat, pat dry, and rub with pepper. Peel and chop the onion. Heat the oil and sear the meat on both sides. Add the onion and olives, and sauté for 5 minutes. Add the broth and simmer for 30 minutes.

Place tomatoes into boiling water briefly (do not cook them), then plunge into cold water. Skin and core them, cut them into 8 wedges and add to meat 10 minutes before the end of the cooking time.

Remove the cooked meat, sprinkle with salt, and keep warm. Strain the cooking liquid through a sieve. Mix the flour with the sour cream and use the mixture to thicken the gravy.

Steak with Olives

Ingredients

2 large rib-eye steaks (1 lb 5 oz each)

1 onion

4 tbsp vegetable oil

15 pimento-stuffed Spanish olives

freshly ground pepper

3 cups chicken broth

2 tomatoes

1 tbsp all-purpose flour

⅓ cup sour cream

salt

Preparation

Soak the porcini mushrooms in boiling water for 20 minutes. Drain and chop. Set aside.

Heat the oil in a shallow pan, and cook the beef for a few minutes on each side. Remove from pan. Sauté the onion and garlic for a few minutes, then add all mushrooms and cook over high heat until soft.

Add the wine and stock, bring to a boil, and then simmer for 10 minutes. Remove from the heat, add parsley, and season with salt and pepper.

Serve the beef with mushrooms and polenta; sprinkle with extra chopped parsley.

Ingredients

1 ⅔ oz porcini mushrooms, dried

¼ cup olive oil

2 ½ lb rump or fillet steak, cut into 6 pieces

1 yellow onion, chopped

2 cloves garlic, crushed

11 oz shiitake/button mushrooms, mixed

¼ cup red wine

1 cup beef stock

2 tbsp parsley, chopped

parsley, chopped; extra

salt and pepper

Seared Beef with Mushrooms, Garlic and Basil Polenta

Serves **6–8**

Preparation

Place beef on a wire rack set in a flameproof roasting dish or tin. Brush beef with 1 tablespoon oil and sprinkle with black pepper to taste. Bake for 1–1 ¼ hours for medium-rare or until cooked to your liking.

For vegetables: place potatoes, pumpkin or parsnips and onions in a large saucepan, cover with water and bring to a boil. Reduce heat and simmer for 3 minutes, then drain. Arrange vegetables in a baking dish and brush with ¼ cup oil.

Bake at 420 °F/Gas Mark 7, turning once during cooking for 45 minutes or until vegetables are tender and browned.

To make gravy: transfer roast to a serving platter, cover with foil and rest for 15 minutes. Stir wine or stock, mushrooms, tarragon and black pepper to taste into meat juices in a roasting dish or tin and place over medium heat. Bring to a boil, stirring to loosen sediment, then reduce heat and simmer until sauce reduces and thickens. Slice beef and serve with vegetables and gravy.

Oven

Conventional oven: 420 °F

Gas oven: Mark 7

Ingredients

3 lb piece fresh round beef

1 tbsp olive oil

freshly ground black pepper

Roast vegetables

6 large potatoes, halved

6 pieces pumpkin or 3 parsnips, halved

6 onions, peeled

¼ cup olive oil

Family Roast

Mushroom gravy

1 cup red wine

or beef stock

2 oz button mushrooms, sliced

½ tsp dried tarragon

Serves **4**

Preparation

To make the marinade, crush the garlic with the salt, then mix with the rest of the marinade ingredients in a non-metallic bowl. Score each piece of pork a few times with a sharp knife, add to the marinade and turn to coat. Cover and refrigerate for 4 hours, or overnight, turning occasionally.

Preheat the oven to 400 °F/Gas Mark 6. Fill a deep roasting tin halfway with boiling water and place the pork on a rack over the top, ensuring that the meat does not touch the water. Brush the pork with half the marinade and roast for 30 minutes.

Reduce the heat to 350 °F/Gas Mark 4. Turn the pork over and brush with the remaining marinade. Roast for another 30 minutes until the pork is cooked through and tender. Slice into ½ in thick pieces to serve.

Ingredients

1 lb 2 oz rindless boneless pork loin, cut into 2-in wide pieces

For the marinade

2 cloves garlic

1 tsp salt

2 tbsp light soy sauce

3 tbsp sugar

1 tbsp rice wine or medium dry sherry

½ tsp Chinese five-spice powder (optional)

1 tsp hoisin sauce

1 tbsp clear honey

Cantonese Honey-glazed Pork

Preparation

Remove the fat and skin from the pork, rinse under cold running water, pat dry and cut into 10 1-inch slices. Season with pepper.

Rinse the sage, pat it dry, and place 2 leaves on each piece of meat.

Cut the slices of pancetta in half and place 1 piece on each medallion. Wrap each in a slice of bacon. Arrange on skewers, alternating meat and olives.

Brush with oil, place over a hot grill or under a preheated broiler. Grill or broil for 15 minutes, turning occasionally.

Florentine Pork Medallions

Ingredients

2 small pork fillets (10 oz each)

freshly ground pepper

20 sage leaves

5 thin slices pancetta

10 thin slices lean smoked bacon

20 stuffed olives

3 tbsp olive oil

Preparation

Place the ham in a large saucepan and cover with water. Bring to a boil, then simmer for 10 minutes. Drain, cover with fresh water, then add the onion, carrots and herb bundle. Simmer for 1 hour or until the vegetables are tender. Leave to cool in the cooking liquid for 30 minutes.

Preheat the oven to 375 °F/Gas Mark 5. Transfer the ham to a roasting tin. Strain and reserve all the cooking liquid, then add 5 tablespoons to the tin. Combine the mustard and marmalade, then spread over the joint. Bake for 30 minutes, basting twice. Allow to cool for 15 minutes before carving.

To make the sauce: Heat the butter in a saucepan, then fry the shallots for 5 minutes. Stir in the flour and cook for 2 minutes, stirring. Stir in 1 ⅕ cup of the reserved liquid and simmer for 2 minutes. Stir in the milk and cook for 20 minutes, stirring often. Add the capers, parsley, mustard and cream. Heat through, season and serve with the meat.

Ingredients

1 lb 11 oz piece boneless smoked or unsmoked ham

1 onion, halved

2 carrots, sliced

herb bundle of thyme, parsley sprigs and a bay leaf

1 tsp English mustard powder

2 tbsp orange marmalade

For the sauce

¼ cup butter

2 shallots, chopped

3 tbsp all–purpose flour

1 scant cup full-fat milk

1 tbsp capers, rinsed, dried and chopped

2 tbsp chopped fresh parsley

1 tsp Dijon mustard

2 tbsp heavy cream

salt and black pepper

Baked Ham with Caper Sauce

Serves **6**

Preparation

Rinse lamb under cold running water, pat dry. Make small slits in the flesh, and insert garlic slivers using a sharp knife tip. Heat the oil and sear the meat on both sides.

Purée the tomatoes and season with rosemary, salt and pepper. Bring to a boil briefly. Place tomato mixture in casserole, add the lamb and place in the oven. Add the peas shortly before the meat is cooked and simmer for a maximum of 10 minutes. Remove the meat, debone, and cut into slices.

Ingredients

1 leg of lamb (3 lb 5 oz)

12 cloves garlic, peeled

6 tbsp olive oil

14 oz can tomatoes with juice

pinch of dried rosemary

salt, freshly ground pepper

2 cups fresh (or frozen) green peas

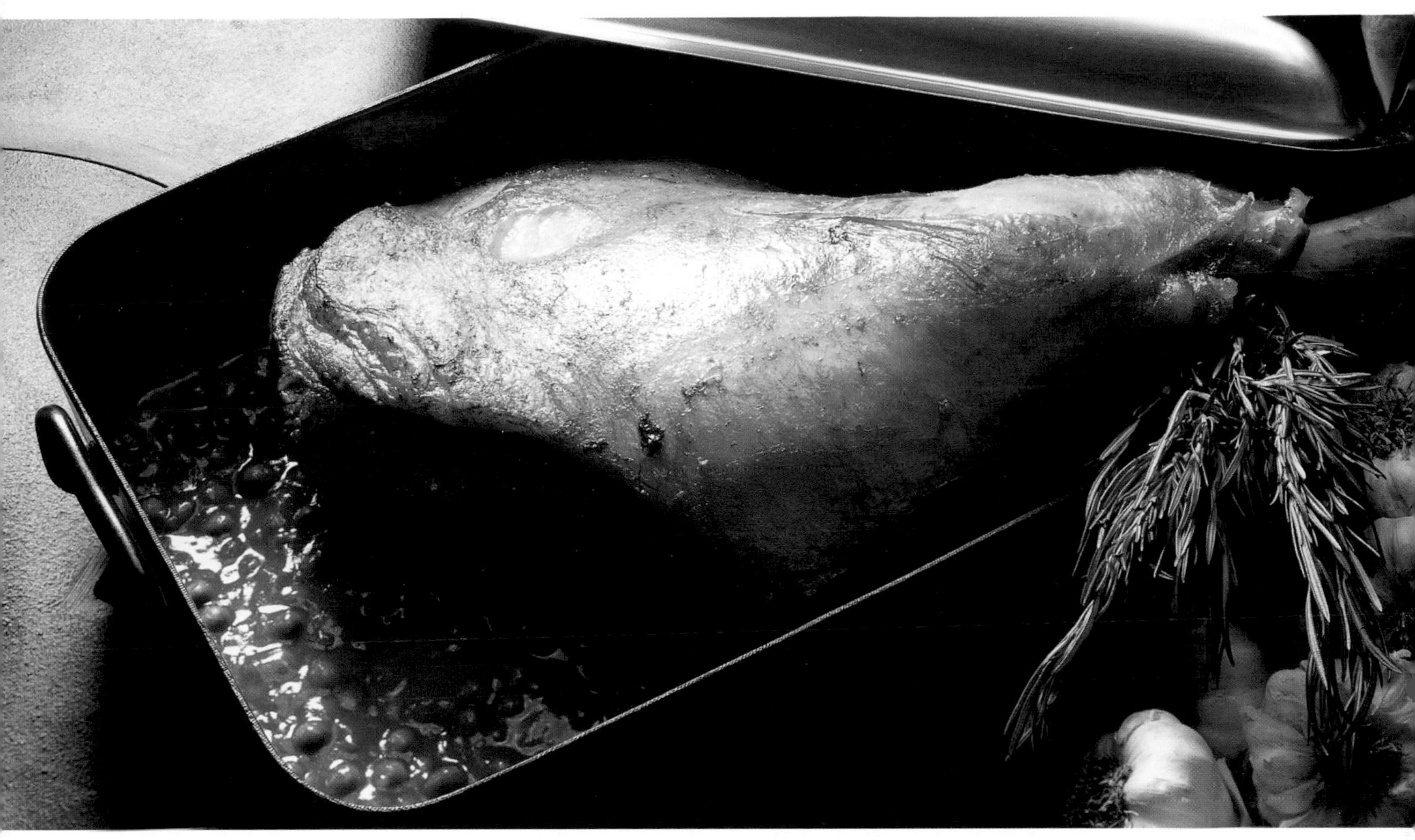

Tuscan Leg of Lamb

Oven

Conventional oven: 375 °F (preheated)

Fan-assisted oven: 350 °F (not preheated)

Gas oven: Mark 2–3 (not preheated)

Roasting time: about 1 ½ hours

Serves **4–6**

Preparation

Preheat oven to 350 °F.

Lightly grease an ovenproof dish with butter, and arrange the potato slices in overlapping rows on the dish. Season with salt, pepper, garlic and nutmeg in between each layer.

Mix the flour and Parmesan cheese into the cream, and pour over the potatoes. Sprinkle with extra Parmesan cheese, and bake in the oven for 40–45 minutes, or until potatoes are cooked.

To make the pesto: place the mint, parsley, garlic, pinenuts and cheeses in the bowl of a food processor. Process, until finely chopped. Add the olive oil in a steady stream, with processor still running. Season with salt and pepper, and set aside.

Preheat chargrill plate, or pan, and grease lightly with a little oil. Season lamb with extra salt and pepper to taste. Chargrill the lamb on both sides for approximately 5–10 minutes or until done to your liking.

Serve the lamb, sliced diagonally, on a bed of creamy potatoes with the mint pesto.

Chargrilled Lamb
with Mint Pesto and Creamy Potatoes

Ingredients

1 lb potatoes, thinly sliced

4 lamb backstraps (or fillets) (14 oz)

1 clove garlic, crushed

1 tsp nutmeg

1 tbsp all–purpose flour

⅓ cup Parmesan cheese, grated

1 cup cream

2 tbsp Parmesan cheese, grated (extra)

salt & freshly ground black pepper

For the Mint Pesto

1 cup mint leaves

½ cup parsley leaves

2 cloves garlic

½ cup pinenuts, toasted

3 tbsp Parmesan cheese, grated

3 tbsp Pecorino cheese, grated

⅓ cup olive oil

salt & freshly ground black pepper

Serves **4**

Preparation

Preheat oven to 350 °F.

Heat the oil in a large pan, add garlic and lamb cutlets, then brown on medium heat for 2–3 minutes on each side.

Add wine and cook for 2 minutes. Mix the tomato paste with the beef stock and add to the lamb cutlets. Add the rosemary, black olives and pepper.

Transfer lamb to a casserole dish and bake for 30–40 minutes.

Ingredients

1 tbsp olive oil

2 cloves garlic, minced

8–12 lamb cutlets, depending on size

⅗ cup white wine

⅗ cup beef stock

2 tbsp tomato paste

2 sprigs rosemary, roughly chopped

⅓ cup black olives

black pepper, freshly ground; to taste

Lamb Cutlets with Olives & Rosemary

Preparation

Rinse the meat under cold running water and pat dry. Carefully rinse the sage and pat dry. Place one leaf of sage on each piece of meat. Top with folded slices of ham and secure with a cocktail stick. Season with salt and pepper, then dust with flour.

Heat the oil and sear the meat on both sides for 2–3 minutes. Remove from the pan and keep warm. Pour the broth and vermouth into the pan and deglaze. Season again if desired.

Veal Schnitzel with Ham and Sage

Ingredients

8 veal schnitzel slices (about 3 oz each)

8 sage leaves

8 slices Parma ham

freshly ground pepper

salt

1–2 tbsp all-purpose flour

3 tbsp olive oil

1 cup veal consommé

2 tbsp dry vermouth

Additionally

cocktail sticks

meat & poultry

Serves **4**

Preparation

Preheat the oven to 350 °F.

Boil the potatoes until soft. Drain, then mash, or purée, and add the olive oil, chopped capers and 1 tablespoon roasted garlic. Mix well, season with salt and pepper (to taste) and set aside until ready to serve.

Heat 2 tablespoons of olive oil in a pan, and brown the veal on both sides, until well sealed. This will take approximately 5 minutes. Remove the veal from the pan, and place on a rack in a baking dish. Rub veal with 1 tablespoon of roasted garlic and 1 tablespoon of thyme leaves, season with salt and pepper, and add half the wine and stock to the baking dish.

Roast in the oven for 20 minutes, or until veal is cooked to your liking. Wrap in foil and let rest for 10 minutes.

Add remaining stock, wine and thyme to the pan-juices and cook over medium heat for 5 minutes, until the liquid has reduced by a third.

Serve veal on a bed of mashed potatoes with pan-juices and sage leaves.

Ingredients

1 ½ lb potatoes, peeled, chopped

½ cup olive oil

1 tbsp capers, chopped

2 tbsp roasted garlic purée

salt

black pepper, freshly ground

2 tbsp olive oil

2 lb rack of veal

2 tbsp thyme leaves

1 ⅕ cup white wine

1 ⅕ cup chicken stock

Rack of Veal with Thyme
on Roasted Garlic Mashed Potato

Preparation

Peel and dice the onion. Dip the tomatoes in boiling water (do not allow them to cook), transfer them to cold water and skin them. Scoop out the pulp, and dice. Peel, wash, and dice the potatoes.

Rinse the chicken under cold running water, pat dry, and season with salt, pepper, and garlic.

Heat the oil in a flameproof casserole or Dutch oven and sauté the chicken until brown all over. Add the diced onion and potatoes and continue frying. Add the diced tomatoes, the poultry stock, rosemary, and parsley. Place the pan in the oven (see below for temperatures and cooking times).

Remove the meat from the oven when cooked through and season to taste with salt and pepper. Serve with ciabatta and salad leaves.

Oven

Electric oven: 375 °F (preheated)

Fan-assisted oven: 350–375 °F (not preheated)

Gas oven: Mark 3 (not preheated)

Cooking time: around 40 minutes

Baked Chicken Italian Style

Ingredients

1 onion; 2 beefsteak tomatoes

2 cups small potatoes

1 lb 12 oz skinless chicken pieces

(boned legs, thighs and breast)

salt and freshly ground pepper

1 clove garlic, peeled and crushed

4 tbsp olive oil

1 scant cup chicken broth

3 small sprigs rosemary

1 tbsp chopped parsley

Tip

Serve with a rosé wine from Piedmont or with chianti.

Preparation

Place the pineapple slices in a sieve over a bowl to catch the juice and leave to drain. Chop the pineapple into chunks. **Rinse** the chicken legs under cold running water and pat dry. **Combine** the soy sauce with the chili sauce, pineapple juice, pepper, and curry powder. Brush the chicken legs with the mixture and leave to marinate for several hours, turning and basting from time to time.

Cut the bell peppers into halves, remove the stalks, seeds and white parts. Wash and cut into strips. **Clean** the green onions, wash them, and cut across into 1-inch pieces. Mix the bell peppers, onions, and pineapple pieces and spoon the mixture into an oval earthenware ovenproof casserole dish rinsed with water.

Add the remaining pineapple juice and the cashew nuts. Sprinkle with salt, add the chicken legs to the casserole, pour over the marinade and place the dish on the middle shelf in a cool oven. See below for roasting times and temperatures.

Remove the casserole from the oven, and stir the canned baby corn into the vegetables. Switch off the oven.

Return the casserole to the warm oven for 10 minutes.

Season to taste and serve.

Marinated Chicken Drumsticks

Ingredients

5 canned pineapple slices

4 chicken drumsticks (about 7 oz each)

3 tbsp soy sauce

3 tbsp chili sauce

6 tbsp pineapple juice

½ tsp freshly ground pepper

1 tsp curry powder

1 red and 1 green bell pepper

1 bunch green onions (scallions)

3 tbsp cashew nuts; salt

1 cup canned baby corn

Oven

Conventional oven: 400–425 °F

Fan-assisted oven: 375–400 °F

Gas oven: Mark 4

Roasting time: 60–70 minutes

Preparation

Rinse the chickens under cold running water, pat dry, and cut into quarters. Season the meat with salt and pepper and sprinkle with flour.

Heat the oil in a skillet, brown the chicken pieces all over, and remove from the pan. Strain the juices.

Melt half of the butter in the pan. Clean the mushrooms, rub with paper towel, rinse if necessary, pat dry, and fry gently with the drained pearl onions. Add the red wine. Add the rinsed, chopped thyme, bayleaf, and the cream.

Return the chicken pieces to the pan and cook over low heat for approximately 25 minutes.

Dot with the remaining butter, stir, and adjust the seasoning.

Serve with rice and salad.

Ingredients

2 oven-ready chickens (2 ½ lb each)

salt and freshly ground pepper

2 tbsp all-purpose flour

3 tbsp vegetable oil; 5 tbsp butter

2 cups button mushrooms

¾ cup pearl onions

2 cups red wine

1 bayleaf; 2–3 sprigs of thyme

1 scant cup heavy cream

Coq au vin—Chicken in Red Wine

Preparation

Rinse the chicken breasts under cold running water, pat dry, and rub with salt and pepper. Wrap each chicken breast piece in a thin slice of ham and secure with a cocktail stick.

Heat the oil in a skillet and gently sear chicken breast on both sides for 15 minutes. Remove from the skillet and keep warm.

Deglaze the pan with Marsala wine, mix with crème fraîche and boil briefly. Season the meat with salt, remove the cocktail sticks, and transfer the chicken to the Marsala sauce. Reheat for 2 minutes before serving.

Serve with Risotto and mixed leaf salad.

Ingredients

4 small chicken breast fillets (4 oz each)

freshly ground pepper

chopped sage

4 thin slices raw ham

2 tbsp clarified butter

3–4 tbsp Marsala wine

⅔ cup crème fraîche

salt

Chicken Breast in Marsala Sauce

Tip

French bread and green salad go well with this rich chicken dish.

Preparation

For the salad: quarter the bell pepper, remove the stems, seeds, and white ribs, wash and cut into strips. Trim the tips of the zucchini, wash and cut into slices. Mix both ingredients with the parsley, chopped green onions, and chopped chili peppers.

Combine the oil and vinegar, season with salt, pepper, and sugar and mix with the salad ingredients.

Rinse the chicken fillets under cold running water and pat dry.

Mix the tomato paste with sambal oelek and olive oil and spread this mixture only on one side of the fillets.

Heat the oil, place the fillets, mixture side down in the pan and cook on low heat for 5 minutes (there is a danger of burning on higher heat). Spread the other side of the fillets with the spice mixture and turn them over. Cook for an additional 10 minutes, or until done. Arrange the fillets beside the salad and serve.

Serve with warm pita or creamed potatoes.

Ingredients

For the salad

1 red bell pepper; 4 zucchini

2 tbsp minced flat-leaf parsley

4 tbsp chopped green onions (scallions)

2 tsp chopped red chili pepper

4 tbsp oil; 2 tbsp chopped tarragon leaves

salt; freshly ground pepper; pinch of sugar

For the chicken breasts

4 chicken breast fillets (6 oz each)

5 tbsp tomato paste

2 tsp sambal oelek

(spicy Indonesian condiment)

4 tbsp olive oil, 4 tbsp vegetable oil

Spicy Chicken Breasts with Salad

Preparation

Rinse the turkey fillets under cold running water and pat dry. Make slits in the sides of the fillets.

Heat the milk, pour it over the diced white bread, and leave to soak. Add the egg, season with salt, pepper, and sage then knead into a ball.

Divide the stuffing between the turkey fillets, pushing it into the slits, and secure with cocktail sticks or kitchen twine.

Heat the oil in a roasting pan and brown the turkey breasts all over. Add the chicken broth, and place the pan on the middle shelf of the oven.

Peel the kohlrabi, wash, and cut into strips. After 30 minutes of roasting, add the kohlrabi, the cocktail onions, and the diced bacon to the turkey breasts and continue roasting all the ingredients together. Stir frequently.

Oven

Electric oven: approximately 375 °F (preheated)

Fan-assisted oven: approximately 350 °F (not preheated)

Gas oven: Mark 2–3 (not preheated)

Cooking time: approximately 70 minutes

Baked Turkey Breast

Ingredients

1 lb 12 oz turkey breast fillet

1 scant cup milk

8 slices crustless white bread

1 medium egg

1 tsp dried sage

freshly ground pepper

salt

2 tbsp oil

1 scant cup chicken broth or consommé

2 kohlrabi

1 cup bottled cocktail onions

⅓ cup diced bacon

Tip

Serve with French bread or parsleyed potatoes.

Preparation

Rinse the turkey drumsticks in cold running water, pat dry, and rub with salt, pepper, and dried herbs. Peel and crush the garlic and rub it all over the turkey drumsticks.

Heat the oil in a pressure cooker. Sauté the drumsticks, add the red wine, and cover the pressure cooker with its lid. When sufficient liquid has evaporated (after about 1 minute) position the pressure cooker on 11. Cook the drumsticks for 30–35 minutes on position 11. Remove the pressure cooker from the heat source, slowly and gradually reduce the pressure regulator and open the pressure cooker. Remove the drumsticks and arrange them on a heated serving platter.

Deglaze the cooking liquid with the crème fraîche and simmer for a minute. Season with salt and pepper and serve as a gravy for the meat.

Serve with Ratatouille, French bread, pasta, or rice.

Turkey Drumsticks Provençal Style

Ingredients

2 turkey drumsticks (1 lb 7 oz each)

salt and freshly ground pepper

chopped dried herbs; 2 cloves garlic

2 tbsp olive oil; 1 scant cup red wine

⅔ cup crème fraîche

Preparation

Rinse the turkey fillets under cold running water, pat dry, and cut into small cubes. Cut the peppers in half, remove the stalks, white parts, and seeds. Wash and dice the peppers.

Heat the oil in a Dutch oven and sauté the turkey, potato, and paprika cubes. Add the tomato chunks, chicken broth, and chili sauce, then simmer for 30 minutes, stirring occasionally.

Deseed the chili peppers and cut them into small pieces.

Shortly before the end of cooking time, season well with the chili, sambal oelek, salt and pepper.

Serving suggestion: Serve this dish with French bread or pita, salad, and fruity white wine.

Ingredients

14 oz turkey breast fillets

3 bell peppers (red, yellow, and green)

14 oz potatoes

3 tbsp vegetable oil

1 14-oz can chopped tomatoes

1 cup chicken broth

1 small bottle mild chili sauce

2 small red chili peppers,

sambal oelek to taste

salt and freshly ground pepper

Spicy Turkey Chili

FISH & SEAFOOD

Preparation

Boil the rice for the rice cookies in salted water for 35–40 minutes. Strain and cool. Clean the leek thoroughly and cut into thin slices.

Melt 2 tablespoons of the butter and fry the leek. Remove the leek and let it cool. Mix the rice, leek, and egg then season with salt and pepper. Melt the rest of the butter and use a tablespoon to transfer small portions of the rice to a skillet. Press the rice portions flat, brown them on both sides for 2 minutes, and keep warm.

Rinse the fish fillet in cold running water, pat dry, and sprinkle with lemon juice. Season with salt and pepper, pressing the pepper into the fish.

Melt the butter, fry each side for around 8 minutes, and keep warm.

For the sauce: peel and finely cut the shallots. Melt half the butter and sauté the shallot until it is glazed. Beat in the flour then moisten with the wine.

Bring the sauce to a rolling boil. Add the rest of the butter, the mustard, and cream, and let the sauce simmer for around 3 minutes. Season with salt and pepper.

Arrange the fillets together with the wild rice cookies and sauce on a plate.

Serving suggestion: Radicchio salad or leeks.

Ingredients

For the wild rice cookies

6 tbsp wild rice; 4 cups salted water

½ leek; 3 tbsp butter

1 egg; salt; freshly ground pepper

For the fish

4 red snapper fillets (around 7 oz),

1 lemon, juice squeezed; 4 tbsp butter

For the champagne-mustard sauce

2 shallots

4 tbsp butter

1 tbsp all-purpose flour

1 cup dry white wine

2 tbsp champagne mustard

1 cup heavy cream

Red Snapper Fillet
with Wild Rice Cookies

Serves **6–8**

Preparation

Make the rouille first. Purée the garlic, chili pepper and cilantro with salt in a mortar until they form a smooth paste. Stir in the mayonnaise and oil and add some extra salt to taste. Set aside in the fridge.

Cut the fish in 2-inch pieces. Rinse the shrimp (having removed the shells and black veins) thoroughly under running water. Cut the squid into 2-inch slices. Remove the mussels from their shells, but leave a few intact for the garnish.

Heat the oil in a thick-bottom saucepan and sauté the onion for 4 minutes or until soft. Add the fennel seeds, cook briefly, then add the wine and stir in the tomatoes and herbs. Bring to a boil and let the sauce thicken without a lid for 5 minutes. Add the fish, squid, mussels and shrimp; put the lid back on and simmer for 5–6 minutes or until the shrimp has turned pink and all the fish is cooked. Stir often. If needed, season the dish and serve with the rouille in a separate bowl.

Mediterranean Fish Dish

Ingredients

2 lbs mixed fish and shellfish
(e.g. cod, snapper, mackerel, shrimp, squid),
prepared and ready to cook
1 lb ready-to-cook mussels in their shells
2 tbsp olive oil
1 onion, minced
1 tsp fennel seeds
1 cup dry white wine
14 oz tomatoes, diced
salt and pepper

Ingredients for the rouille

2 cloves garlic, minced
1 small red chili pepper,
seeded and finely chopped
3 tbsp fresh cilantro, finely chopped
3 tbsp mayonnaise
1 tbsp olive oil
pinch salt

Preparation

Break the pasta into finger-length pieces and cook in boiling salted water to which oil has been added. Cook the pasta al dente according to the instructions on package. Drain in a colander. Rinse fish fillets under cold running water, pat dry, drizzle with lemon juice, pat dry again and sprinkle with salt. Bring the broth to a boil with wine, add the fish and cook for 6 minutes.

Place the pasta in a buttered deep ovenproof dish and arrange the fish on top. Grate the cheese and sprinkle a third of it over the fish. Wash the leeks and fennel and slice them into rings. Skin, core and quarter the tomatoes. Melt the butter, and sauté the leeks and fennel for 10 minutes. Add the tomato and briefly heat through. Add the heavy cream. Season the vegetables with salt and pepper and arrange them over the fish. Sprinkle with remaining cheese and dot with butter if desired. Place in oven.

Oven

Conventional oven: 400 °F (preheated)

Fan-assisted oven: ca. 180 °F (preheated)

Gas oven: Mark 3–4 (preheated)

Baking time: around 30 minutes

Sardinian Ziti with Fish

Ingredients

8 oz macaroni; 1 tbsp vegetable oil

14 oz fish fillet (e.g. cod or red snapper)

lemon juice; salt; ½ cup fish broth

½ cup dry white wine

7 oz Gouda cheese

1 leek; 2 fennel bulbs; 5 tomatoes

3 tbsp butter; 1 scant cup heavy cream

freshly ground pepper,

4 tsp butter flakes

Remarks

Ziti is a special type of Italian pasta; not as long as spaghetti, but thicker and hollow. If you cannot find ziti, use ridged penne or rigatoni instead.

fish & seafood

Serves **6**

Preparation

Season the fish fillets with salt and pepper, and dust each piece with flour.

Heat the oil in a non-stick pan, add the fish and cook gently for 10–15 minutes until cooked and tender, turning once. Keep warm.

Meanwhile, cut the toast into small pieces.

Heat the butter in a second pan and fry the pieces of bread until golden, turning occasionally.

Stir in the parsley and shrimp, then season to taste with salt and pepper. Cook gently for a few minutes, until piping hot, stirring occasionally.

Place the fish fillets on serving plates and spoon the shrimp and croutons over the top.

Serve immediately, garnished with fresh herb sprigs.

Fillet of Plaice with Shrimp

Ingredients

18 plaice fillets,
each weighing about 2 oz
salt and freshly ground black pepper
3 tbsp all-purpose flour
½ cup olive oil
4 slices toast
5 ½ oz butter
1 sprig fresh parsley, chopped
7 oz cooked, shelled shrimp
fresh herb sprigs, to garnish

Serves **4**

Preparation

Bring the wine and ½ cup water to a boil with the bay leaf, thyme, salt and peppercorns in a saucepan.

Add the fish to the liquid and simmer for about 20 minutes until cooked and tender. Using a spatula, place the fish on a warmed dish, cover and keep warm in a low oven.

For the mustard sauce: strain the fish stock, retaining 1 cup liquid. Bring to a boil in a pan.

Mix the crème fraîche with the flour in a bowl and gradually stir into the fish stock. Cook gently for about 5 minutes, stirring, then mix the egg yolk with the milk or cream and mustard. Add to the pan, stirring.

Stir in the butter and season with pepper and sugar to taste.

Sprinkle the fish with chopped parsley, garnish with lemon and tomato slices and serve with the sauce spooned over.

Haddock in Mustard Sauce

Ingredients

1 cup dry white wine
1 bay leaf
a pinch of dried thyme
1 tsp salt
10 peppercorns
4 haddock cutlets or fillets (6 oz each)
½ cup crème fraîche
1–2 tbsp all-purpose flour
1 egg yolk
2 tbsp milk or cream
2 tbsp mustard
3 tbsp butter
freshly ground white pepper
chopped fresh parsley, to sprinkle
lemon and tomato slices, to garnish
sugar, to taste

Serves **6**

Preparation

Shell the shrimp and remove and discard their heads and tails. Cut down the back of the shrimp, devein, then cut in two lengthways. Set aside.

Cut the perch or cod fillets into even, bite-sized pieces and set aside.

Heat 3 tbsp oil in a pan and fry the onion and peppers for 3 minutes. Add the garlic, zucchini and tomato pulp. Mix well and cook for 5 minutes, stirring occasionally.

Add the bouquet garni, stock and salt and pepper (to taste). Cover and cook over a moderate heat for 20 minutes, stirring frequently.

Heat the remaining oil in a separate pan and sear the shrimp all over evenly for 3 minutes. Season with salt and pepper. Drain on absorbent paper towel and keep warm in the oven.

Place the fish in a steamer. Season with salt and pepper; steam, covered, over a pan of boiling water for 5 minutes.

Remove and discard the bouquet garni from the vegetable mixture and blend to a smooth purée with a hand-held electric mixer.

Serve the cooked fish and shrimp with the vegetable purée sauce, garnished with the fresh chervil.

Ingredients

18 raw king shrimp

1 lb 12 oz ocean perch or cod fillets

5 tbsp olive oil

1 onion, finely chopped

½ red pepper, seeded and thinly sliced

½ green pepper, seeded and thinly sliced

1 clove garlic, finely chopped

1 tomato, skinned, seeded and chopped

1 bouquet garni (parsley, thyme, bay leaf)

salt and freshly ground black pepper

1 cup fish stock

1 zucchini, sliced

fresh chervil, to garnish

Ocean Perch and King Shrimp Duet

Serves **6**

Preparation

Cut each sea bass fillet in two, to obtain 4 small fillets per person. Season with salt and pepper and set aside.

Mix together the lemon juice, aniseed and 2 tbsp oil in a bowl. Add the fish fillets and leave to marinate for 1 hour, turning occasionally.

Bring the milk to a boil in a saucepan. Add a little salt and the fennel slices and cook for 5 minutes. Drain, then spread out to dry on a clean tea-towel.

Drain the fish marinade into a frying pan. Add the shallots and tomatoes and cook for 3 minutes, then add the stock. Reduce over a high heat for 5 minutes, stirring occasionally.

Add the cream and bring to a boil. Remove from the heat and blend until smooth with a hand-held electric mixer. Check the seasoning.

Strain the sauce through a fine sieve, pressing through with a spoon to obtain a smooth texture. Keep warm in a bowl over a pan of boiling water.

Preheat a cast-iron griddle and grease with the remaining oil. Sear the fish fillets on each side, then place in an ovenproof dish and finish cooking in a preheated oven at 400 °F/Gas Mark 6 for 10 minutes.

Meanwhile, cook the fennel in the butter in a pan until lightly colored, stirring occasionally. Season with salt and pepper.

To serve: top the fennel with the fish and sauce. Garnish with dill sprigs.

Ingredients

6 small sea bass, filleted
2 tbsp butter
juice of ½ lemon
1 tbsp aniseed
3 tbsp olive oil
2 cups milk
3 fennel bulbs, sliced
2 shallots, finely chopped
2 tomatoes, skinned, seeded and chopped
1 ¼ cup fish stock
⅞ cup heavy cream
salt and freshly ground black pepper
fresh dill sprigs, to garnish

Grilled Sea Bass
with Fennel and Aniseed

Serves **4**

Preparation

Sprinkle the fish fillets with lemon juice, roll up and secure with cocktail sticks.

In a saucepan, bring the wine, stock, butter and salt to a boil, add the sole roulades and cook for about 12 minutes.

Just before the fish is fully cooked, add the shrimp to heat through. Remove the fish and shrimp from the stock, place on a plate, cover and keep warm.

Boil the stock rapidly to reduce to about ⅓ its original volume, then whisk in the cream and egg yolks.

Remove the sauce from the heat and season with salt and pepper to taste.

Serve the roulades and shrimp with the sauce poured over. Garnish with watercress sprigs, lemon slices and red pepper strips.

Serving suggestion: Serve with boiled new potatoes, mangetout and asparagus.

Lemon Sole Roulades
in a White Wine Sauce

Ingredients

8 lemon sole fillets, weighing about 1 lb 5 oz in total
4 tbsp lemon juice
1 cup white wine
1 cup stock
1 tbsp butter
1 tsp salt
3½ oz cooked, shelled shrimp
½ cup heavy cream
2 egg yolks
freshly ground white pepper
fresh watercress sprigs, lemon slices and red pepper strips, to garnish

fish & seafood

Serves **4**

Preparation

Cut the bacon slices in half lengthways, then again in half crossways.

Place a piece of the fish onto each slice of bacon and roll the bacon around the fish.

Thread the bacon and fish rolls onto large skewers, alternating with slices of pepper, mushroom and bay leaves.

Brush the kabobs with oil and arrange on a grill pan.

Preheat the grill to hot and cook the kabobs for 10–15 minutes, turning frequently to prevent the kabobs from over-cooking.

Meanwhile, heat the wine, vinegar and shallots in a small saucepan until boiling. Cook rapidly to reduce by half.

Add the herbs and lower the heat.

Using a fork or small whisk, beat the butter bit by bit into the hot wine mixture, whisking rapidly until the sauce becomes thick. Season to taste with salt and pepper.

Arrange the kabobs on a serving plate and serve with a little of the sauce spooned over and the remainder in a separate jug.

Monkfish and Pepper Kabobs

Ingredients

8 slices of lean bacon, rind removed

1 lb monkfish,

skinned and cut into 1-in pieces

1 small green pepper,

seeded and cut into 1-in pieces

1 small red pepper,

seeded and cut into 1-in pieces

12 small mushroom caps

8 bay leaves

3 tbsp vegetable oil

½ cup dry white wine

4 tbsp tarragon vinegar

2 shallots, finely chopped

1 tbsp chopped fresh tarragon

1 tbsp chopped fresh chervil or parsley

1 cup butter, softened

salt and freshly ground black pepper

Tip

When making the sauce, it is important to whisk briskly, or it will not thicken sufficiently.

Serves **4**

Preparation

Defrost the shrimp according to the package directions. Rinse the tomatoes under cold running water, pat dry, halve, and cut off the stems. Cut the yellow bell pepper in half; remove the stems, seeds, and ribs. Rinse the pepper, cut into large pieces and scald in salted boiling water for 3–4 minutes. Drain in a colander and peel off the skin. Peel and cut 4 garlic cloves in half. Rub the mushrooms with paper towel to clean them and thread all the ingredients on metal or wooden skewers.

Peel 2 garlic cloves and press them through a garlic press. Melt the butter and add the pressed garlic, lemon juice, salt, and sugar. Baste the kabobs with this mixture. Broil the kabobs on a broiler pan lined with aluminum foil or grill them on a barbecue, allowing at least 2 minutes on each side.

Serve with boiled rice.

Shrimp Kabobs

Ingredients

For the kabobs

12 pieces of frozen bay shrimp

(headless, with shells)

4 salad tomatoes

1 yellow bell pepper; salted water

4 garlic cloves; 8 button mushrooms

For the garlic butter

2 garlic cloves; 2 tbsp butter

1 tbsp lemon juice; salt; sugar

Tip

The kabobs can also be cooked in a non-stick skillet.

Serves **4**

Preparation

Make the marinade by mixing chili powder, oregano, garlic, grated orange and lime peel in a bowl. Add the shrimp and mix.

Marinate in a covered bowl in the refrigerator for one hour.

Drain the shrimp and sauté on both sides on a pre-heated coal or barbecue grill until they turn color, about 1 minute.

Mix the papaya and the mint in a bowl. Spoon the shrimp onto the plates, distribute the papaya mixture on top and place the lime wedges and finely cut peppers alongside and serve.

Ingredients

2 lbs medium-sized raw shrimp, unpeeled

9 oz papaya, cut into pieces

2 tbsp fresh mint, finely chopped, lime wedges

Spanish peppers, cut

Orange marinade

2 tbsp mild chili powder

2 tbsp fresh oregano, finely chopped

2 cloves garlic, pressed

1 tsp grated orange peel

1 tsp grated lime peel

¼ cup orange juice; ¼ cup lime juice

barbecued shrimp with Spanish pepper

Barbecued Shrimp with Spanish Pepper

Serves **3–4**

Preparation

Place the mussels, onion, celery, garlic and water (or white wine) in a large saucepan.

Cook the mussels on medium heat until they open; shake the pan occasionally. This ensures that the mussels cook evenly. Add pepper to taste. Just before serving, stir some butter and parsley through the dish. Discard any unopened mussels.

Mussels à la Marinière

Ingredients

2 lbs ready to cook mussels in their shells

1 small onion, in rings

1 stalk celery, sliced

1 clove garlic, minced

4 tbsp water or white wine

1 tbsp butter

1 tbsp finely chopped parsley

pepper

Preparation

Melt the butter for the sauce, stir in the flour and cook until golden-brown, and then stir in the broth and milk. Continue stirring so no lumps form. Bring the mixture to a boil. Peel the onion, stick the bayleaf and cloves in it, add it to the sauce, and cook on low heat for another 15–20 minutes. Strain the sauce through a sieve and stir in the Swiss cheese. Mix the egg yolk with the heavy cream to thicken the sauce. Keep warm. Cut the coconuts in half and drain out the milk. Clean and rinse the fennel and carrots and slice thinly lengthwise.

Melt the butter and fry the vegetables for 3 minutes. Rinse the tarragon and add it with the lobster tails and shrimp to the vegetables frying for 2 minutes. Add the vermouth and fry for another 3 minutes. Arrange the vegetables, lobster tails, and shrimp in the coconut halves. Leave the cooking liquid to thicken slightly, stir it through the Mornay sauce and pour over the filled coconut halves. Grate the cheese, sprinkle it over the coconut halves, place them in a baking pan and bake in the center of the oven.

Oven

Conventional oven: 425 °F (preheated)

Fan-assisted oven: 400 °F (preheated)

Gas oven: Mark 4–5 (preheated)

Baking time: around 5 minutes

Filled Coconut Halves

Ingredients

For the Mornay sauce

5 tbsp butter; ⅔ cup all-purpose flour

1 cup meat broth

2 cups milk; 1 onion

1 bayleaf; 2 cloves

½ cup grated Swiss cheese

2 medium egg yolks

4 tbsp heavy cream

For the coconuts

2 coconuts

2 fennel bulbs; 4 carrots

3 tbsp butter; 1 bunch tarragon

16 peeled lobster tails

1 cup peeled shrimp

1 cup dry vermouth

3 oz mild cheddar cheese

Preparation

Peel and slice the bananas, sprinkle them with lemon juice, and mix with the curry powder and cooked rice.

Heat the lobster in butter for around 2 minutes, add the shrimp.

For the cocktail sauce: mix the tomato ketchup, heavy cream, and brandy then season with salt, pepper, sugar, and tabasco.

Place the banana rice on a pre-heated platter, arrange the lobster and shrimp on top, and pour over the cocktail sauce.

Lobster with Banana Rice

Ingredients

For the banana rice

2 small bananas; 1–2 tbsp lemon juice

2 tsp curry powder

⅔ cup cooked rice grains

1 cup lobster (from a frozen lobster defrosted and cooked)

2 tbsp butter; ⅔ cup bay shrimp

For the cocktail sauce

1–2 tbsp tomato ketchup

½ cup heavy cream

1 tbsp brandy

freshly ground pepper

a few drops tabasco

salt and sugar

Serves **4**

Preparation

Whisk the egg yolks over water in a bain-marie (with a double boiler) until you have a mayonnaise-like substance.

Add the melted butter in a thin trickle, while still beating and season with salt, pepper, nutmeg and lemon juice.

Stir the cream in carefully and keep the mayonnaise warm. Remove the mussels from their bottom shells. Heat the spinach in a small pan and place a little bit of spinach in every shell. Place the mussels on the beds of spinach and cover them with the mousseline sauce.

Bake under the broiler until they form a golden brown crust, then serve immediately.

Florentine Mussels

Ingredients

2 lbs mussels in their shells (cooked à la marinière, with the top shells removed)

7 oz fresh spinach, cooked, chopped finely and mixed with 1 oz butter

For the mousseline sauce

4 egg yolks

4 tbsp water

1 tbsp whipped cream

salt, pepper; nutmeg

juice of 1 lemon

Serves **6**

Preparation

Halve the lobsters lengthwise and remove meat; cut into chunks.

Melt the butter and sauté the onions until tender. Add the flour and stir over a low heat for 2 minutes.

Gradually add the milk and allow the sauce to thicken. Add the liqueur and simmer for 2 minutes then stir in the cheese and mustards.

Spoon a little of the sauce into the lobster shells, add the lobster and coat with the remaining sauce. Sprinkle with breadcrumbs and dot with butter.

Grill until brown and bubbling.

Serve immediately.

Grilled Creamy Lobster

Ingredients

3 medium, cooked lobsters

4 tbsp butter or margarine

1 small onion, chopped

3 tbsp flour

1 ½ cups milk

3 tbsp cherry liqueur

2 tbsp grated mild Cheddar cheese

2 tsp French mustard

½ tsp English mustard

breadcrumbs

butter

Serves **4**

Preparation

Soak the cloud ear for 1 hour. Cut the lobster in half lengthwise and remove the meat, reserving the shells. Cut the meat into 8 equal portions and drop in boiling water. When the surface of the meat whitens, immediately drain and plunge into ice water. Drain again and wipe dry.

Wash the shells thoroughly and boil in lightly salted water until they turn red.

Cut the shiitake (or brown) mushrooms into thin strips. Cut the cloud ear, carrot, and asparagus into 1½ inch long slivers.

Preheat the oven to 400 °F.

Combine the bonito stock and all the vegetables in a soup pot and bring to a boil over high heat. Season with soy sauce and mirin, then boil for about 3 minutes until the vegetables are just tender. Pour in the beaten egg in a circular motion to cover, and stir gently. Cover with a plate which fits down inside the pan and sits directly over the food, then turn off the heat (this ensures even heat and flavor distribution). Let stand for 2–3 minutes and then drain.

Return the lobster to the shells. Top with the egg mixture and place in the preheated oven. When the surface of the egg mixture is lightly browned, remove the lobster from oven, transfer to plates, and serve.

Stuffed Spiny Lobster

Ingredients

1 dried cloud ear mushroom

2 live (1 lb) spiny lobsters

4 fresh shiitake mushrooms, washed and destemmed (or 4 fresh brown mushrooms, washed and trimmed)

¼ medium carrot

2 stalks green asparagus, trimmed

7 tbsp bonito stock (dashi)

1 tbsp light soy sauce

1 tbsp mirin

3 eggs, lightly beaten

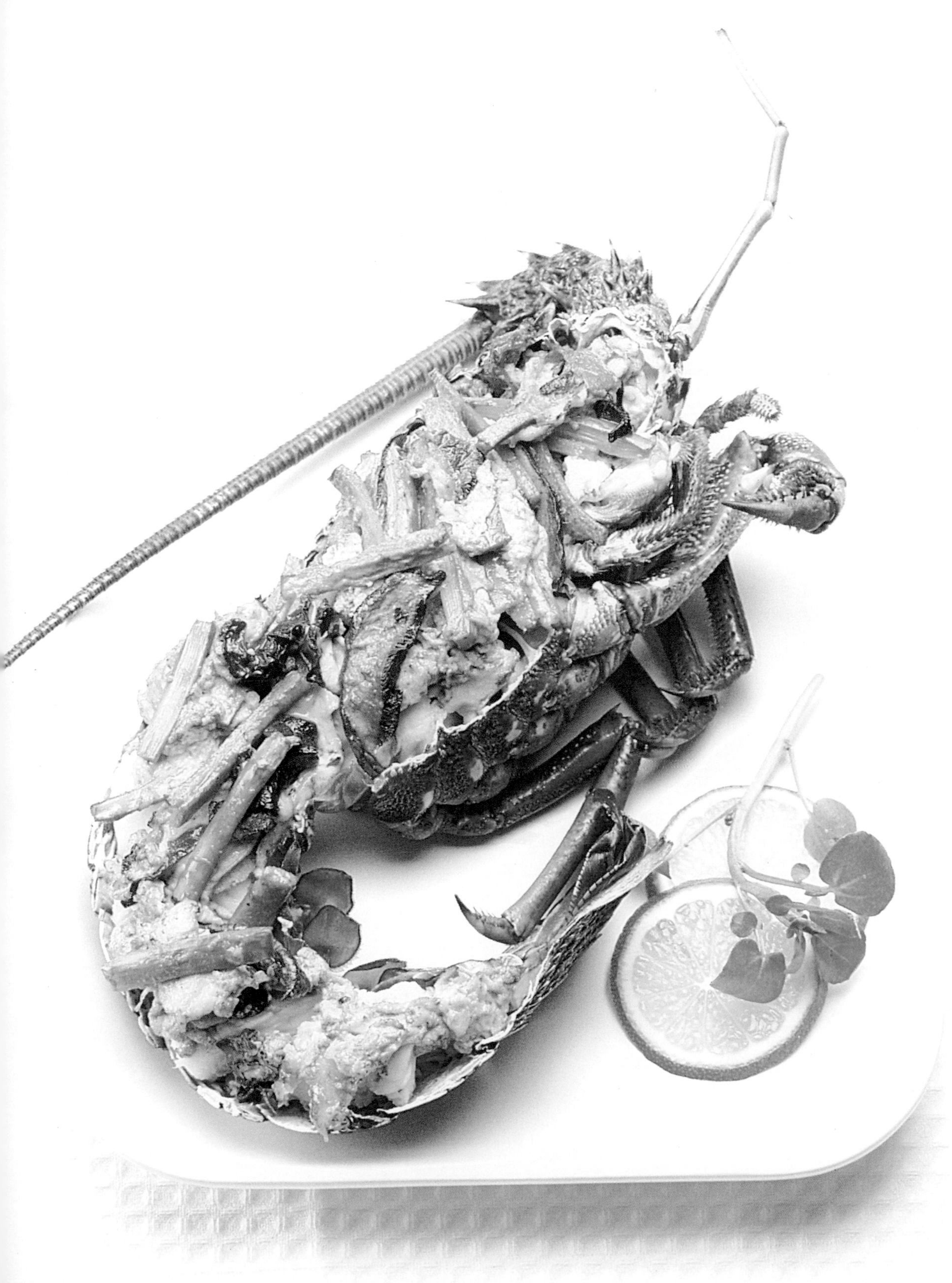

Serves **4**

Preparation

To make pesto: place mint leaves, almonds, garlic and lime juice in a food processor (or blender) and process until finely chopped. With machine running, slowly add oil and make a smooth paste.

Place lobster on a baking tray, spread pesto over meat and bake for 15–20 minutes or until lobster is cooked.

Serving suggestion: This dish is perfect for a special occasion meal. Start with an antipasto platter—purchase the ingredients from the delicatessen section of your supermarket. Accompany lobster with boiled new potatoes tossed with olive oil and black pepper and a salad of assorted lettuce and chopped fresh herbs. Finish the meal with a good quality ice cream topped with a tablespoon of your favourite liqueur.

Oven

Conventional oven: 400 °F

Gas oven: Mark 6

Ingredients

2 uncooked lobster tails, halved lengthwise

Mint pesto

1 bunch fresh mint

4 tbsp almonds, toasted

1 clove garlic, crushed

¼ cup lime juice

¼ cup olive oil

Lobster in Mint Pesto

DESSERTS

Preparation

To make the mixture: combine the sifted flour with the baking powder and cocoa powder in a mixing bowl. Add sugar, vanilla sugar, egg, butter, and ground hazelnuts. Mix the ingredients using the dough hooks on the mixer, starting slowly then increasing the speed to maximum. Turn onto a work surface and knead until smooth and elastic. Leave in a cool place. Use the dough to make four cake layers.

Roll out one-fourth of the dough onto the base of a 10-inch greased, springform pan and prick the surface with a fork. Bake each base without the springform in a 375–400°F preheated oven for 10–15 minutes. Unmold onto a plate. Repeat with the other three portions of dough. Cut one layer into 16 triangles. Allow to cool.

To make the frosting: melt the chocolate and creamed coconut in a bain-marie (water bath). Brush the 16 triangles with the frosting. Mix the powdered gelatin with water and leave to soak, following the instructions on the package. Rinse the lime in hot water, dry it, and rub the rind with the corners of the sugar lumps.

Heat the softened gelatin with the sugar lumps in a small pan, stirring until the gelatin has dissolved. Add the lime juice. Whip the cream until almost stiff, add the lukewarm gelatin solution, then whip the cream until stiff. Fold in the sifted powdered sugar.

Fill a piping-bag fitted with a star-shaped nozzle with some of the whipped cream.

Divide the top cake layer into sixteen sections and pipe out whipped cream whirls, starting in the middle and working outward towards the edge. Spray or brush the other two rounds with the rest of the whipped cream and build up the cake using the three layers. Arrange the iced triangles diagonally in the whipped cream whirls, and decorate with half-slices of lime.

Chocolate-Lime Torte

Ingredients

For the dough

1 ½ cups all-purpose flour

2 level tsp baking powder

2 tsp cocoa powder; ¾ cup sugar

1 package vanilla sugar; 1 egg; ¾ cup butter

2 scant cups ground hazelnuts

For the frosting

2 oz chocolate; 2 tsp creamed coconut

For the filling

3 heaping tsp unflavored gelatin

3 tbsp cold water; 1 untreated lime

5 sugar lumps; 7 tbsp lime juice

5 tbsp heavy cream; 1 ⅓ cups powdered sugar

For the decoration

lime slices, halved

12 pieces

Preparation

Break the chocolate bar into pieces and melt with the butter or margarine in a bain-marie (water bath) over a low heat until smooth. Sift the flour, baking powder, and baking soda over a mixing bowl and combine with the sugar, vanilla sugar, and salt.

Add the eggs, coffee, and melted chocolate. Beat with the dough hook until soft and pliable. Finish by beating in the grated chocolate.

Fill two 6-cup muffin pans with the mixture and place on the middle shelf of a preheated 375°F oven. Bake for approximately 25 minutes.

Remove from the oven and leave in the pans for 10 minutes. Unmold onto a wire rack to cool.

Whip the double cream. While whipping, add the whisky and flavor the cream with vanilla sugar and sugar. Spread this frosting over the muffins.

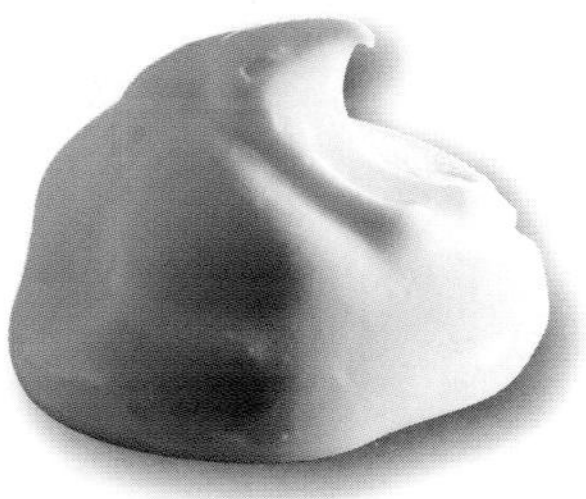

Chocolate-Whisky Muffins

Ingredients

5 ½ oz plain baking chocolate

⅓ cup butter of margarine

2 cups all-purpose flour

2 level tsp baking powder

½ level tsp baking soda

⅓ cup sugar; 1 package vanilla sugar

pinch of salt; 2 eggs

2 tsp strong coffee; 4 tbsp whisky

4 tbsp grated chocolate

For the cream frosting

1 cup heavy cream

2–3 tbsp whisky

1 package vanilla sugar

pinch of sugar

desserts

Preparation

Bring the sugar and water to a boil. Let the syrup boil once to dissolve the sugar. Leave to cool. To make the dough, whisk the egg yolks with the hot water until light and fluffy. Gradually add two-thirds of the sugar and whisk until creamy. Mix the flour with the cornstarch and baking powder, sift over the egg mixture, and fold in. Grease the base of an 8-inch springform pan and line with nonstick baking paper. Transfer the dough to the base and place in a preheated 400°F oven. Bake for 25–30 minutes.

Blend the syrup with the brandy. Prick the pastry base a few times with a fork, sprinkle over the liquid, cover and leave to cool.

To make the truffle paste: bring the cream and milk to a boil. Stir in the instant coffee, the dark chocolate and the mocha chocolate. Continue stirring until melted. Add vanilla sugar and salt. Remove the pastry from the base and crumble it over a bowl. Use the mixer to blend the warm truffle paste with the pastry crumbs. Put the bowl in a cool place.

Divide the mixture into approximately thirty pieces. Wrap each piece around a cocktail cherry. Dip the balls in sprinkles and refrigerate until required.

Choc-cherry Truffles

Ingredients

For the sugar syrup

2 tbsp sugar; 2 tbsp water

For the dough

2 eggs; 3 tbsp hot water; 3 tbsp sugar

4 tbsp all-purpose flour; 4 tbsp cornstarch,

1 level tsp baking powder

1 tsp butter; 4 tbsp brandy

For the truffle paste

2 tsp whipping cream; 2 tbsp milk

2 tbsp instant coffee

3 ½ oz plain baking chocolate

3 ⅓ oz mocha chocolate

1 package vanilla sugar

pinch of salt; about 30 cocktail cherries

1 cup plain chocolate sprinkles

for rolling the truffles in

desserts

Preparation

Caramelize half of the sugar in a pan and stir the caramel through the milk. Add the vanilla, whipping cream and salt to the caramel milk and bring to a boil.

Beat the egg yolk and the rest of the sugar until frothy. Pour the hot milk and whipping cream mixture over it and heat to a maximum of 185 °F.

Run the entire mixture through a sieve and fill four ovenproof dishes or soup bowls with the cream.

Place the dishes (or bowls) in a dish filled with water and slide into the oven. Cooking time is 20 minutes.

Poach the mixture until the cream stiffens.

Remove the cream from the oven and chill.

Sprinkle the top of the chilled cream with light brown sugar and place in the oven with the upper heat on the highest setting, or in the middle position under the grill. Bake the crème slowly until the sugar caramelizes.

Decorate the crispy upper crust of the crème with orange, grapefruit and melon segments.

Garnish the dessert with mint leaves and serve immediately.

Crème Brûlée

Ingredients

¼ cup sugar; ⅔ cup milk

½ tsp vanilla extract

¾ cup whipping cream

5 egg yolks

⅔ cup light brown sugar

pinch of salt

Tip

You can check whether the crème is ready with a knitting needle: when you poke it in the middle of the crème, it should come out clean.

Preparation

Beat the egg yolks and one-third of the sugar with an electric mixer until foaming. Beat the egg whites in a bowl until stiff, gradually adding one-third of the sugar. Refrigerate the egg whites. Beat the whipping cream with the rest of the sugar until stiff, and refrigerate. **Soften** the gelatin according to the package instructions and dissolve in the cherry brandy. Melt the white chocolate in a bain-marie (water bath) over gently boiling water on low heat, stirring constantly. Add a third of the egg yolks and the gelatin, stirring. Lightly fold in a third of the whipped cream and then a third of the beaten egg whites. Transfer the mixture to a bowl or individual dishes and refrigerate. **Melt** the milk chocolate in a bain-marie (water bath) over gently boiling water on low heat, stirring constantly. As with the white chocolate, add a third of the egg yolks, then a third of the whipped cream, followed by Grand Marnier and a third of the egg whites.
Slide this over the white chocolate mousse in the bowls with an upturned spoon, then return to the refrigerator. Melt the dark chocolate in a bain-marie (water bath) over gently boiling water on low heat, stirring. Add the remaining egg yolks and the brandy. Fold in the remaining whipped cream and egg whites. **Spoon** into bowls with an upturned spoon and refrigerate for at least another 2 hours.

Three-colored Chocolate Mousse

Ingredients

6 medium egg yolks
9 tbsp superfine sugar
6 medium egg whites
1 ¼ cups heavy cream
4 tsp unflavored gelatin
2 tbsp kirsch
3 oz white baking chocolate
3 oz milk baking chocolate
3 oz plain baking chocolate
2 tbsp Grand Marnier
2 tbsp brandy

Preparation

Beat the egg yolks with the egg, vanilla sugar, sugar, and salt into a thick, creamy mixture. Quickly fold in the mascarpone and stir only until it is incorporated, or the mixture will coagulate into a buttery consistency.

Soften the gelatin in water according to the manufacturer's instructions. Heat the brandy and 2 tablespoons Amaretto. Dissolve the gelatin in this mixture and stir it through the mascarpone mixture. Refrigerate until lightly set.

Stir the remaining Amaretto with the espresso. Place the cake base on a cookie sheet, pour the espresso coffee over it and sprinkle with cocoa powder.

Beat the egg whites whilst gradually adding sugar until they form stiff peaks. Carefully fold the egg white into the mascarpone mixture. Use the mixture to cover the espresso-soaked cake base. Refrigerate for 2–3 hours before serving.

Before serving sprinkle the tiramisù with extra cocoa powder.

Ingredients

2 medium egg yolks
1 medium egg
½ tsp vanilla sugar
4 tsp sugar
1 pinch salt
1 cup mascarpone
2 tbsp unflavored gelatin

2 tbsp brandy
4 tbsp Amaretto
½ cup strong espresso coffee, cold
1 sponge cake base
cocoa powder
2 medium egg whites
4 tsp sugar

Tiramisù

Preparation

Beat the egg yolks, sugar, and marsala wine or port over boiling water until mixture is thick but still liquid.

Pour it into sundae glasses or dessert bowls and sprinkle with chocolate flakes.

Serve immediately with vanilla wafers, if desired.

Ingredients

4 medium egg yolks

3 tbsp sugar

⅓ cup Marsala or port

chocolate flakes

vanilla wafers to serve

Zabaglione

desserts

Preparation

Prepare the vanilla mousse with milk according to the directions on the package and let cool for at least 2 hours.

Rinse the pears with hot water, pat dry and halve them lengthwise. Remove the cores and stems. Cut the half-pears lengthwise again into very thin slices and divide them over 4 plates. Sprinkle 1 tablespoon port or apple juice on each portion. Use a spoon to place little balls of mousse on the pear slices.

Sprinkle the rest of the port or apple juice over the dessert.

Pear Carpaccio with Vanilla Mousse

Ingredients

1 package vanilla mousse

1 cup milk

4 ripe pears, about 8 oz

6 tbsp port or apple juice

Variation

Serve the pear carpaccio with chocolate mousse instead of vanilla mousse.

Tip

Stew the pear slices for about 3 minutes in white wine or port, let cool in their own juices and divide them over the plates.

Serves **6–8**

Preparation

Clean the rhubarb and cut into pieces. Clean and wash the gooseberries. Place the rhubarb and gooseberries with a bit of water in a pan and bring to a boil.

Drain well in a sieve and let cool. Wash the strawberries and remove the crowns.

Prepare the gelatin according to the instructions on the package. Stir the lemon zest, sugar, vanilla extract and lemon juice together with the quark (20% fat) and creamy quark until the sugar is totally dissolved. Prepare the gelatin in a pan on low heat.

Stir a few tablespoons of quark crème through the gelatin and and then stir the dissolved gelatin throughout the quark mixture. Crumble the meringue and spoon it through the mixture.

Line a 10x4 in baking mold with aluminum foil, spoon a layer of cream over it and part of the strawberries, gooseberries and rhubarb and cover this with a layer of cream. Continue making layers and finish with a layer of crème.

Refrigerate the crème for at least 4 hours.

Invert the molds and serve with fresh fruit and meringue, if desired.

Ingredients

⅓ lb rhubarb

⅓ lb gooseberries; ½ lb strawberries

1 envelope unflavored gelatin

zest of one organic lemon

2 oz sugar; 1 tsp vanilla extract

2 tbsp lemon juice

2 lbs 30 oz quark (or low-fat cottage or "curd" cheese) (20% fat),

½ lb creamy quark

3 meringue rounds (1 oz each)

if desired, serve with fresh fruit and meringue

Quark Crème

Tip

You can also freeze the quark crème into an ice pudding. In that case, leave out the gelatin.

Preparation

Drain the Morello cherries, reserving the juice. Stir the cornstarch into the cold juice. Bring the rest of the juice to a boil in a saucepan and thicken with the diluted cornstarch. Stir in the cherries and add sugar to taste. Cool, stirring occasionally. Soften the gelatin according to the package instructions.

Beat the yolks with the whole eggs, powdered sugar, and port wine. Heat this over boiling water until thick. Stir the gelatin into the port wine cream over low heat until dissolved.

Dip the base of the bowl containing the mixture into cold water to cool, stirring occasionally to prevent a skin from forming. Beat the whipping cream until stiff and lightly fold in.

Divide the cherry mixture into individual dishes or spoon into a large glass bowl. Add the port wine cream and garnish with chocolate flakes.

Portwine Jellycream

Ingredients

1 ¾ cups canned Morello cherries, drained

1 heaping tbsp cornstarch

2–3 tbsp cold cherry juice

sugar

For the portwine jellycream

2 tbsp unflavored gelatin

cold water

2 medium egg yolks

2 medium eggs

6 tbsp sifted powdered sugar

½ cup port wine

1 cup whipping cream

chocolate flakes

Preparation

Peel the oranges and grapefruit as you would an apple. Remove all the "white skin." Cut the fruit from the sections. Cut the melon in half horizontally and remove the seeds with a spoon. Slice the melon halves into sections. Remove the peel and cut the sections into blocks. Divide the melon cubes, pieces of orange and grapefruit over four plates.

Roast a bit less than half the grated coconut in an ungreased frying pan until golden brown. Bring the milk and the sugar to a boil, stir in the semolina and the rest of the grated coconut through the mixture and cook for about 4 minutes. Remove the semolina mixture from the heat and beat with a mixer until frothy, about 3 minutes. Flavor the mixture with lemon juice and let cool.

Pour the lukewarm coconut froth over the fruits and sprinkle with the roasted coconut.

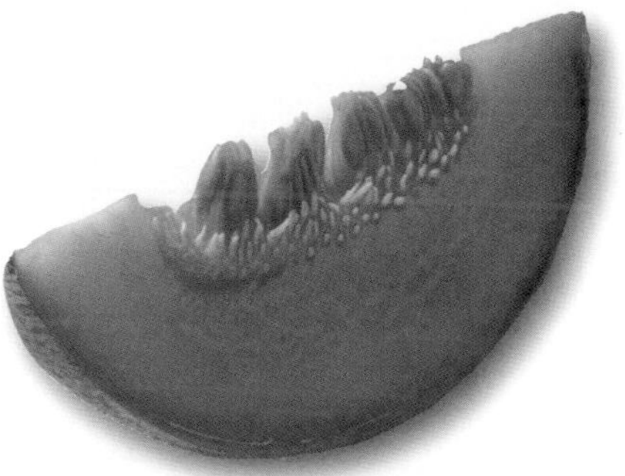

Fruit Mix with Coconut Froth

Ingredients

2 oranges; 1 pink grapefruit

1 gallia or similar melon

½ cup grated coconut

2 cups milk

⅓ cup sugar

3 tbsp wheat semolina

1–2 tsp lemon juice

Variation

Substitute half of the milk with whipping cream or canned coconut milk. This will give the coconut froth an even more pronounced flavor.

Tip

You can also use coconut liqueur to flavor the semolina mixture.

Serves **4**

Preparation

Combine the flour, sugar, egg yolks, and milk. Melt the butter and stir 1 tablespoon into the batter. Grease a skillet or omelet pan with some of the melted butter and pour in a small amount of batter. Brown the crêpe on both sides and roll it up. Make 5 more crêpes in the same way.

Wash and dry the oranges and remove the zest by rubbing with the sugar lumps.

Heat the remaining butter in a skillet or omelet pan, dissolve the sugar lumps and when they start to brown, add the lemon and orange juice and heat, stirring.

Return the crêpes to the pan and re-heat them in the sauce. Spoon the sauce over the crêpes. Pour the Grand Marnier over the crêpes and set it alight. Sprinkle with thin slivers of almonds.

Crêpes Suzette

Ingredients

1 ½ cups all-purpose flour
2 tbsp sugar
2 medium eggs
1 cup milk
½ cup butter
2 untreated oranges
10 sugar lumps
2 tbsp sugar
2 tbsp lemon juice
½ cup orange juice
3 tbsp Grand Marnier
toasted almond slivers

Serves **6**

Preparation

For the yogurt ice cream: Pour the cognac over the raisins and let soak for 3 hours.

Beat the eggs, honey and vanilla together with a mixer until foamy. Stir in the yogurt.

Beat the whipping cream until stiff, fold it into the yogurt mixture and freeze for 1 hour.

Stir in the raisins and freeze the mixture for another 1½ hours, stirring thoroughly once every 30 minutes. Press the frozen mixture into a round (1½ quart) bowl and freeze for at least another 2 hours.

Let the ice cream stand at room temperature while you prepare the sauce.

For the raisin-wine sauce: Heat the butter and the honey, stirring constantly, until it turns a golden color. Add the white wine, lemon juice and raisins; simmer for 3 minutes as you continue to stir.

Invert the yogurt ice cream on a large dish and sprinkle it with walnuts.

Beat the whipping cream until stiff. Serve the ice cream with the whipped cream and the hot sauce.

Ingredients

For the yogurt ice cream

⅓ cup raisins; ½ cup cognac

3 eggs; 2 tbsp honey

1 tsp vanilla extract

1¼ cup yogurt; 1⅓ cup whipping cream

For the raisin-wine sauce

2⅓ tbsp butter; 3 tbsp honey

½ cup white wine; 1 tbsp lemon juice

approx. ¼ cup raisins

⅕ cup chopped walnuts

½ cup whipping cream

Yogurt Ice Cream
with Raisin-wine Sauce

Variation

Prepare the yogurt ice cream with caramelized walnuts: heat 3 tbsp butter and 3 tbsp sugar in a pan and caramelize ¼ cup walnuts in it.

Tip

You can garnish the dish with halved grapes. The ice cream can also be made in an ice cream maker, which will shorten the freezing time considerably.

Serves **4**

Preparation

Pour the lemon juice into a small pan and add sugar. Heat the mixture over low heat and dissolve the sugar. Cook the mixture until it thickens. Pour into a jug and allow to cool for 20 minutes. Place the syrup for at least 1 hour (or overnight) in the fridge. Cut off the melon skin and remove the seeds.

Cut the fruit flesh into pieces and pour the extra melon juice into a bowl. Scatter finely chopped mint over the melon and mix carefully.

Add the melon juice to the cold syrup. Pour the syrup over the pieces of melon shortly before serving. Sprinkle the melon with grated lemon rind.

Watermelon with Lemon Syrup

Ingredients

juice of 1 lemon

2 ½ tbsp fine crystal sugar

2 ¼ lbs watermelon

1 tbsp mint, finely chopped

grated lemon rind

desserts

Preparation

Wash oranges under hot running water, dry. Peel 3 oranges and set aside.

Thinly peel the lemon, and slice the rind into matchstick strips. Squeeze the oranges and lemon. Pour the juice into a saucepan, add the sugar and the grated orange rind. Reduce the liquid to a syrupy sauce over medium heat.

Peel the figs and cut them in half. Pour the hot orange sauce over the figs and sprinkle with the matchstick strips of lemon rind. Cover with plastic wrap and refrigerate overnight.

Whip the cream with vanilla until semi-stiff. Add sugar to taste. Spoon the whipped cream over the figs and serve ice-cold.

Ingredients

4 untreated oranges

1 lemon

1 cup sugar

12 fresh black figs

1 scant cup whipping cream

1 package vanilla sugar

extra sugar to taste

Figs in Orange Sauce

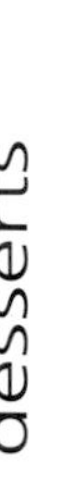

Index

Index